Dress the Show

A Basic Costume Book

By Daty Healy

Foreword by Nellie McCaslin

Illustrated by the Author

NEW PLAYS, INC., ROWAYTON, CONNECTICUT

TABLE OF CONTENTS

FOREWORD v

INTRODUCTION vi

TOWARD A PERMANENT COSTUME COLLECTION . . 1

MATERIALS 3

DYEING AND SURFACE TREATMENT OF FABRICS . . . 4

ACCESSORIES AND TRIMMINGS 6

THE TUNIC 9

SHORT TUNICS 11

LONG TUNICS 13

COSTUME FOR CHINESE WOMAN 15

TROUSERS 17

LONG TROUSERS 19

SHORT TROUSERS 21

VEST DIAGRAMS 23

VESTS 25

BOLERO JACKETS 27

JACKET DIAGRAMS 29

JACKETS 31

ACCESSORIES TO THE BODICE DRESS 33

BODICE DRESS 35

BODICES 39

BODICES AND BLOUSES 41

A Few National Variations 43

THE STRAIGHT SKIRT 45

SEMICIRCULAR SKIRT 47

COATS AND CLOAKS 47

CAPE DIAGRAMS 49

CAPES 51

THREE TRADITIONAL COSTUMES 53

HATS AND HEADDRESSES 55

CAPS AND HALOS 55

CROWNS AND BRIMMED HAT 57

BONNETS 59

HATS BASED ON THE CIRCLE 61

FOOTGEAR 63

FANTASTIC COSTUMES 64

FOUNDATIONS FOR ANIMAL COSTUMES . . . 65

ANIMALS 67

EARS AND THREE MASKS 69

BIRDS 71

INSECTS 73

FLOWERS 75

VEGETABLES AND FRUITS 77

OTHER FANTASTIC CHARACTERS 79

MASKS 83

ORNAMENT AND ACCESSORIES 85

BIBLIOGRAPHY 96

INDEX 97

DEDICATION

To Ruth Robinson Warner,
my best student costumer,
whose energy and resourcefulness
were heightened by her humor

FOREWORD

THE editor of *New Plays for Children* is to be congratulated for adding a book on costume to an expanding list of titles. With the publication of *Dress the Show,* an attractive and useful text is made available to the consumer of school and community theatre productions. The author, Daty Healy, brings to the subject an impressive background in art history, illustration and years of experience in costuming non-professional plays. The result is a practical guide, profusely and charmingly illustrated.

Dr. Healy's emphasis on a permanent costume collection is sound. She advises the building of a wardrobe that can be used again and again by putting garments together in different combinations that require only minor adjustments, accessories or alterations. To this end she has organized the material under such chapter headings as: tunics, trousers, vests, jackets, bodices, capes, hats, and accessories. By following her suggestions the non-professional costumer, operating on a limited budget, can plan wisely for the future while at the same time solving immediate problems.

Dr. Healy provides patterns as well as pictures and she supplies clear directions for making basic garments. Although there are a number of excellent costume books available, most of them are geared to the experienced, if not professional designer. *Dress the Show* speaks to the student, the inexperienced and/or non-professional costumer. The author's simplicity of presentation and her own sense of security should serve to inspire confidence in the most apprehensive reader. This book is a valuable addition to the literature in the field and it will be welcomed by all who are seeking an up-to-date guide to stage costume in the educational and community theatres.

NELLIE McCASLIN
The Program in Educational Theatre
New York University

Past President of the Children's
Theatre Association of America

INTRODUCTION

LET'S FACE IT

A Problem in Mental Arithmetic

Given: A play to produce + very little time — a great deal of experience + a small budget — a library of books on costuming = the need for a compact workbook to help the costumer in educational, community and camp theatre.

Dress the Show is worked out with this problem in mind. It is designed to present in simple form many practical considerations for the costumer on a budget and one who depends upon student helpers and others not experienced in theatrical production. Its point of view is directed toward the building of a permanent costume wardrobe and the understanding of the *basic* costume patterns.

The illustrations are planned to give as many practical examples of historic and national dress as are consistent with the aim of demonstrating in each group of pictures the flexibility of the particular basic garment under discussion. It has been the author's objective to emphasize the types of costumes demanded in educational and community productions. It is hoped that the many excellent books concerned with period styles and national variations will be available for further enrichment of costume problems. The most primary needs for the costumer, however, are: a functional point of view, a practical approach, and an awareness of all resources and help which exist in the community.

Here is the problem. Let's face it.

TOWARD A PERMANENT COSTUME COLLECTION

W HEN ONE is asked to "whip up some costumes for just a simple little play," it is a temptation to think only in terms of immediate necessity and easy solution. Planning for the present in terms of a useful future for costumes will pay large dividends. With this idea in mind, let us think of a permanent rather than a temporary accumulation of costumes.

Just as a wise mother has a box of attic castoffs for children to dress up in, the school, camp and community center should have available a group of costumes simple enough to be translated into Indians, Chinese, peasants, or pioneers with only a few hours' work in alteration, addition of accessories, or subtraction of details. A box of substantial skirts, both straight and circular; a few capes; some simple tunics and trousers, both long and short; jeans, T-shirts, and tights; several bodice-type dresses; blouses; a box of scarves, sashes, and odd pieces of material suitable for draped or tied headdresses; these would create for any group a sound start for the beginning of a permanent costume collection.

While it is easy to lean back on the custom of having each member of the cast furnish his own costume, made under direction, and then take it away after performance, the security of having on hand a few fundamental beginnings for the next play to come up is lost. The advantage of the "attic box" is never achieved.

In order to plan for permanence it is necessary to think of reasonably durable materials, simple, easily altered design (pattern), stitching that can be removed, and accessories which can be exchanged.

MATERIALS

All theatre is illusion. A first thought in all problems of the stage is that one is creating this illusion and not literally reproducing a slice of life. Acting, settings, costumes, and properties all should be a part of the suggested persons and places. Materials used for costumes therefore should *seem* to be brocades or velvet or feathers or fur, but it is not necessary or even desirable at times that they actually be what they suggest. There are many materials which will drape like velvet, have the sheen of satin, or shine like metal. It is for us to find those weaves and textures which most practically simuate the fabrics we have in mind and which will fit into our budget. A list of reasonable and durable materials is presented in a later division of this book. Warning should here be given to the inexperienced costumer against combining authentic garments with costumes constructed for the stage only. The *real* garment often seems ineffective and out of key when surrounded by costumes the material, sewing, and decoration of which are completely theatrical. This is true because stage costumes, particularly historic and national ones, should suggest and emphasize the outstanding characteristics of silhouette and decoration rather than be exact reproductions.

SEWING

It is assumed that the persons for whom this book is

planned have some knowledge of the fundamental principles of sewing and the use of simple patterns. A few hints as to sewing techniques practical for costumes may be helpful to those whose experience has been limited to dressmaking rather than costuming. To the careful seamstress many of these techniques seem casual, if not careless; but she must remember that *effect* is often the main objective, and that distance and lighting obliterate fine finishes and minor details.

It is not necessary, for instance, to match thread to material in color, but only in value. All very dark fabrics can be stitched in black; all very light fabrics, with white; and the in-between shades, with grey or some color near the hue of the fabric. For all costumes of an impermanent character —dance choruses, flowers, etc.—it is folly to spend time in finishing necklines, armholes, and hems. Many of these will have a freshness resulting from a cleanly trimmed edge that is lost in the thickness of binding and facing. This is particularly true of all circular edges. Plackets need not have professional finish unless the garment is intended for continual use. When raw edges are left and trimmed, be sure that the ends of seams are caught so that no splitting at sides or shoulders becomes an embarrassment.

Costume sewing should be done by machine whenever possible, with the exception of hems. A fairly large but firm stitch is best, and the tension should be such that easy ripping for alteration is possible. Double stitching should be used at points of strain, such as armholes, crotch, and waistband, if it is tight. Rows of stitching, if double, should parallel each other, not overlap, for ease in ripping.

Hooks are preferable to snap fasteners and buttons at all places where there is apt to be strain. Garments should fit and fasten firmly, to give the actor as complete comfort and security as possible. This is of particular necessity with costumes for children, who should not be burdened with directions to be careful, or the fear of embarrassment, if seams should split. Loose garments, such as tunics, blouses, full trousers, and cloaks, are easily interchangeable among actors and should be made in small, medium, and large sizes. Tightly-fitting garments, such as the bodice-type dresses, jackets, and vests, must be carefully adjusted to individual body measurements. Whenever possible use drawstrings or elastic, instead of bands, to increase the flexibility of the garments.

PATTERNS

Since it is the plan of this book to present in diagram and illustration various ways in which a simple, easily procured pattern may be made to serve several purposes, only a few general recommendations need be made here.

1. Commercial patterns, such as pajama patterns, should be re-cut out of strong paper, and each piece marked and labeled for adjustment and variation.
2. If the budget allows it, buy patterns in several sizes, small, medium and large. This saves slashing and folding paterns for size adjustments.
3. Styles change rapidly and the pattern offerings with them. It is wise for the costumer to lay in some useful patterns such as quaint night gowns with yokes which make charming story book characters, or interesting smocks, vests, over-alls, or lounge wear with dramatic lines when these are available. Bridal gowns often serve for queens and court ladies.
4. Patterns which any costumer finds repeatedly useful to have on hand are:
   Pajama (Man and Woman)
   Slacks (Man and Woman)
   Vests (Man and Woman)
   Woman's bodice dress
   Woman's blouse (Tailored)
   Woman's blouse (Peasant—low cut)
   Woman's bolero (often part of a combination pattern, *i.e.,* play clothes)
   Woman's gored skirt (four and six gores)
   Woman's circular skirt
   Bridal gowns
   House coats
   Nightgowns with yoke ("Granny" gowns)
   Child's sleeping garment (one piece)
   Snow or Ski suits with helmet
   Capes
   Caps and other head gear: bonnets, Scottish hats, etc.
   Skating costumes

5. Special costume patterns
   Pattern houses usually carry a few "Special Costumes." These also vary from year to year. Here you most often find patterns for Colonial men and women, pioneers (square dancing), western, and animal figures.

So, take your problems to a department store and let McCalls, Butterick, Vogue and Simplicity help you.

MATERIALS

SINCE a general point of view toward the purchase and use of materials for stage costume was expressed in the preceding section, and suggestions for materials appropriate to individual costumes are offered in specific costume description, it remains for us to attack some of the problems connected with fabrics, papers, paints and dyes.

An ever present concern of the costumes is the limited budget. The best defense against this spectre lies in an understanding of the *nature of materials,* resourcefulness, and imagination. The ability to find new uses for old materials, untried uses for new materials, a willingness to experiment and salvage, and a knowledge of what the market offers and at what price—all these will pay dividends.

Just as patterns constantly change, so it is with materials: fabrics, trimmings, and accessories. Gone are the cheap but charming calico prints, the cottons so easy to dye, the colored tarlatans. In their places are the polyester and cotton prints, brushed nylon, nylon net and double knits which have their own limitations and possibilities. The costumer must discover these in terms of his desired effects and know that in two years or five or ten, there will be other fabrics for introduction and use.

As was said in the general discussion of material, our effort in the theatre is to create illusion, and to do this we do not need to be literal in our choice of fabric any more than we need reproductions of actual period rooms or real antiques for properties. It is necessary to discover what fabrics were generally used in a historical period or a national type of costume, and then to approximate the effects of those fabrics as closely as possible. To do this one needs to be discerning about the nature of materials, to know what fabrics will drape well because of the weight or weave, to sense visual similarities of texture between inexpensive and costly materials, and to develop imagination in substituting the cheap for the prohibitively-priced fabrics.

To assist in this appreciation and imagination, the following tables were arranged. It is far from being an exhaustive list but will provide a springboard from which to leap into a sea of fascinating possibilities.

GOOD FABRICS FOR GENERAL USE

Lightweight
  Unbleached muslin
  Sheeting
  Percale
  Seersucker
  Flannelette
  Sateen
  Spun Nylon
  Acetate—Rayon
Heavyweight
  Denim
  Ticking
  Slip cover fabrics
  Drapery fabrics
  Terry cloth
  Velveteen
  Corduroy
  Monk's cloth
Fine
  China silk
  Organdy
  Nylon
  Marquisette
  Curtain nets
Stiff
  Crinoline
  Buckram
  Nylon net
  Canvas
  Felt
  Vinyl
  Coarse curtain net (starched)

FABRICS THAT DRAPE WELL

A. Good heavy folds
  Muslin
  Duvetyne
  Slip cover and Drapery fabrics
  Corduroy
  Velveteen
  Monk's cloth
  Terry cloth

B. Good soft folds
  Sateen
  Voile
  Soft nylons
  Jersey
C. Stiff folds
  Percale
  Sheeting
  Denim starched
  Plastic shower curtain material

SOME SUGGESTED SUBSTITUTIONS

MATERIAL	SUBSTITUTE FOR
Corduroy	
Duvetyne	Velvet
Plush	
Terry cloth	Fur
Duvetyne	

MATERIAL	SUBSTITUTE FOR
Cotton rug yarn	
Wool yarn	Hair or long fur
Frayed jute	
Canvas	
Vinyl	Leather
Leatherette	
Metallic paper	
Silvered leatherette	
Silvered Net	Metal and metal mesh
Silvered Vinyl	
Celastic	
Gum drops	
Hard candies	Jewels
Beads	

DYEING AND SURFACE TREATMENT OF FABRICS

FABRICS rarely come in the exact color one wishes to use. Often one must start with a bolt of unbleached muslin, because it is less expensive to costume a large group by purchasing in large amounts. Indeed, that necessity is often a blessing, because the variation usually attending hand dyeing and dipping gives added vitality and richness to a group of costumes such as it is impossible to achieve if there is repetition of the flat color of already dyed materials. Costumes made of flat-color fabrics are often made much more satisfactory by a quick dipping into another color, or by a surface spray of a lighter or darker value of its own color.

DYEING

White or light materials may be dyed quite easily by using any of the commercial tints and dyes, and by following the directions exactly. There are several all-purpose dyes which are satisfactory for synthetics as well as cottons or silks; others will be effective only for certain fabrics. Be sure you know what you want and get what you need. Many of the newer dyes can be used without boiling, even for deeper shades; and since stage costumes are not subjected to sunlight, and rarely worn for any length of time without re-dipping, the transitory nature of some colors is no limitation.

It is a comfort to know that for the theatre an even dyeing is not necessary. In fact, slight variation enhances the surface of the material under light; and if the material is only lightly pressed, its texture will seem more interesting. Successive quick dippings in two closely related colors such as blue and blue green, with no attempt to completely superimpose one on the other, will create a very rich effect. It must be remembered that colors change both in shade and intensity as they dry, always toward the lighter and duller side of the scales. Therefore, always aim to get a darker value and a brighter color than you want when finished. Only experiment can teach you when to stop dyeing and start drying.

SPRAYING SURFACES

Dye or a thin solution of poster paint may be sprayed on fabrics to change or vary color or texture. Simple paint sprayers such as the Hudson Spray Gun (glass container and hand pump) may be secured at some paint stores or in artist supply shops. Fab-Spray, a textile paint comes in aerosol cans and may be used. This paint will not come out when garment is washed. Dyes aso penetrate the fabric. Thin poster paint when used in a spray gun usually comes out, more or less, when fabric is washed and makes possible another color for another use of the garment. Spraying is often a solution to the difficulty of having to use colors available only in a limited range. For instance, a fabric of too brilliant red can be softened by spraying it with a thin grey dye, or better yet, a pale green. It can also be greyed by spraying it with a darker red dye, or greyed toward the lighter end of the value scale by spraying it with pink or pale green poster-paint solution. This, of course, is true of all colors and their complements.

There are several other ways in which the technique of spraying proves effective:

1. Spraying the surface of a thin flat material such as muslin gives it the effect of a much richer, thicker material. Any color sprayed over another will do this; but by spraying light over dark, as you can do by using the opaque poster paint, you seem to create a pile on a fabric. Cotton often resembles velvet when so treated.
2. By spraying a fabric with a slightly contrasting color, i.e., gold on green or red-violet on violet, you secure something of the irridescence of changeable taffeta.
3. Tone may be graded from light to dark (say, deeper at the hem line) for accent or to give the effect of a "weathered" garment.
4. Since spraying may be done after as well as before the garment is made, it can serve to "highlight" the folds.

SURFACE DECORATION

Patterned fabrics of certain types, particularly for period costumes, are often too expensive for the slim budget or not available except in large cities. It is possible, and fun, to create your own patterns and to paint them on the material you are about to use or on the finished garment if its construction demands accent of that sort. Bandings, edgings, and single units will usually have to be done on the finished garment. Surface patterns are usually more successful if painted in relation to the yardage. Since fine details are lost at audience distance, keep your pattern bold and your treatment broad. Patterns may be drawn on the material or painted freely. It is often a help to use a stencil or a mask with which to establish the regularity of a dominant motif or to secure some accuracy in repetition, and then to add minor details freely; or the entire pattern may be worked out by using several stencils. Fine painting, with mechanically precise edges, is not necessary. Any one of several kinds of paint may be used.

1. Artists' oil paint or acrylics should be used with a fairly dry brush. This is slow-drying and has a tendency to spread, but the colors are rich. Only experimenting on the particular fabric will determine for you the amount of paint and thinner to use.
2. Regular textile paint is excellent but is expensive for mass effects.
3. Gold and silver spray paint may be used with a stencil.
4. Poster paint is generally satisfactory. It is applied with a bristle brush. Success is dependent on securing the proper thickness of the paint, as it will run if too thin and peel off when dry if too thick. Again, experiment will be the only way to find the exact mixture.
5. Dye powder in a starch will create a workable medium.
6. Crayon, ironed into the fabric, is satisfactory for subtle, but not bold, effects.

Large motifs intended to be used for a long time or as decoration for a permanent item in the wardrobe, say a king's cloak, are best worked out by rough *appliqué*. The motifs are first basted on the garment with edges raw, then finished on the sewing machine, using a long stitch.

Stencils may be cut from regular waxed stencil paper for a large job. A heavy paper with paraffin ironed into it (as leaves are waxed) makes a good substitute for commercial stencil paper. Be sure the stencil is pinned firmly to the material. Paint may be brushed across the stencil opening or sprayed on with the spray gun. If spray is used, be sure all parts of the material not to be ornamented are protected by newspaper.

Masking parts of the material with strips of paper to create stripes, and spraying the uncovered areas, is an easy way to secure a single variation of color. Crossing vertical stripes with horizontal stripes by masking will develop the pattern into a plaid. Using strips with varying edges—scallops, rectangular or triangular notches— will suggest many variations on the masking suggestion. Colors superimposed create wonderful and vibrating surprises. Where refinement of technique is not a demand, there is opportunity for free participation of *amateur* textile designers. So here is an opportunity for pleasure and practice in one of the crafts.

ACCESSORIES AND TRIMMINGS

A TOAST to all those removable, transferable, utterly useful, small items which should be a part of every permanent costume collection!

APRONS

The apron, like the bodice, is so often an indispensable accessory to the peasant dress or skirt, and so often used in simple American costume, that it is a great help to have a number of them ready to use as occasions arise. The simple straight apron, gathered into a narrow band with sash ties, is the most practical kind to use for many purposes. Thes may be long and short, perfectly plain, or banded with colors. A number should be sheer and a few heavy. As the collection grows with the accumulation of performances and gifts, you ought to find one or two of the fancier tea-apron type making an appearance. You may want a few flowered print aprons. There seems to be a use for each one, not once but many times a year, in an active group. Therefore, this is one accessory for which it will pay to buy good material and to make well.

SASHES, SHAWLS, KERCHIEFS

A costumer with a long range of vision will make her scraps from costume cuttings into long scarves or sashes. She will buy and dye an occasional extra yard of fabric to be used for a shoulder shawl or triangular head kerchief. She will collect from students and friends discarded bandanas and mufflers, and pack them all carefully in boxes to await the calls of peasant, pirate, frontiersman, farmer, or bandit. Knitted shawls, Spanish shawls, flowered shawls, and even lightweight baby blankets, may be donated if needs are announced. A shawl in a costume is worth two in an attic!

BELTS AND CORDS

Belts of all sorts—leather or cloth, woven, beaded, braided, linked, or embroidered—no matter how shabby for street wear, can be salvaged for stage use. A plea for gifts of these will usually bring in a number of surprises. You can make your own of vinyl, burlap, leatherette, felt, and flannel, with simulated buckles of silvered cardboard. However you secure them, save them, for they serve many masters.

Drapery departments and theatrical-supply houses usually carry cotton "cable cord" in white and several colors which makes excellent girdling for long tunics of all sorts. This may be dyed easily and is interesting if touched with gold or silver paint. Other drapery trims will solve many of the cord and tassel needs. Small, soft clothesline can be braided or twisted for cord. Scraps of flannelette braid easily. So — don't hunt or borrow — collect!

BUTTONS, BEADS, AND COSTUME JEWELRY

Here come the gypsies! But there is no dismay on your part if you have a box of discards that will glitter. Ornamental buttons which have escaped the collector or have been too common for his grasp; old chips, buckles, pins, necklaces, plastic ornaments, and beads of all sorts, though valueless to others, will be priceless to you. And don't forget that plumbers' supplies are quite effective under stage lights and at audience distance. Brass chains and curtain rings glitter like gold. Washers and screw eyes make beautiful necklaces. Hardware can be helpful on stage as well as behind it.

TRIMMINGS

Save ribbons, laces, edgings, and ruffles! They trim hats and hair and aprons and gowns. A pantalette today —a cuff tomorrow. And with this box of souvenirs pack away all the artificial flowers which may be strewn in your path. They bloom again on stage .

COSTUME PROPS FOR CREATIVE DRAMATICS

For any group concerned with creative dramatics, a collection of accessories is valuable. A hat or an apron, a sash or a shawl, is enough to transform an every day costume to the semblance of a character. Often a prop of this sort destroys self consciousness and makes a young actor immediately "the other person."

1. COMPOSITE DIAGRAM OF LONG AND SHORT TUNIC
(SCALE - 1" = 1')

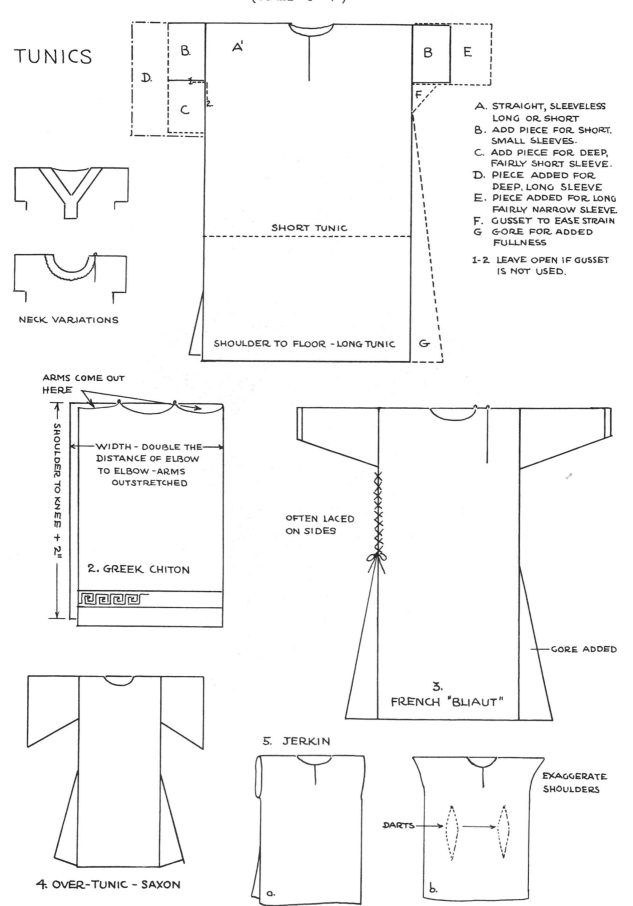

TUNICS

A. STRAIGHT, SLEEVELESS LONG OR SHORT
B. ADD PIECE FOR SHORT, SMALL SLEEVES.
C. ADD PIECE FOR DEEP, FAIRLY SHORT SLEEVE.
D. PIECE ADDED FOR DEEP, LONG SLEEVE
E. PIECE ADDED FOR LONG FAIRLY NARROW SLEEVE.
F. GUSSET TO EASE STRAIN
G GORE FOR ADDED FULLNESS

1-2 LEAVE OPEN IF GUSSET IS NOT USED.

SHORT TUNIC

SHOULDER TO FLOOR - LONG TUNIC

NECK VARIATIONS

ARMS COME OUT HERE

SHOULDER TO KNEE + 2"

WIDTH - DOUBLE THE DISTANCE OF ELBOW TO ELBOW - ARMS OUTSTRETCHED

2. GREEK CHITON

OFTEN LACED ON SIDES

GORE ADDED

3. FRENCH "BLIAUT"

4. OVER-TUNIC - SAXON

5. JERKIN

a.

DARTS

EXAGGERATE SHOULDERS

b.

THE TUNIC

THE TUNIC, a simple, rectangular, sheathlike robe, is probably the most basic of all garments. Its origin was in the Greek chiton, so far as the development of costume in Western civilization is concerned, but it has its counterpart in all the Near Eastern and Oriental cultures. From the simple tunic, as illustrated, have come the long gown and eventually the bodice dress, the blouse, the jacket, and the coat. Cut at first like the kimono nightgown, either sleeveless or with very short, wide sleeves, and in both long and short styles, it was developed so that there were many variations in sleeve lengths and shapes, in neck openings and trims. Gores were added for extra fullness, and various lacings and buttonings were devised to improve the fit.

PATTERNS (See diagrams opposite)

The accompanying illustrations show a few basic forms of the tunic:

1. A COMPOSITE DIAGRAM of the simple tunic is drawn to a practical scale for reproduction. This may be used sleeveless or with any of the indicated sleeve lengths and widths for various purposes. For instance: short with sleeve B for Biblical shepherds, long with sleeve D for Biblical patriarchs. Since a loose tunic was usually girdled, allowance in length must be made for blousing.

2. THE GREEK CHITON (a short one is shown here) is a simple fold of material which was originally pinned on the shoulders at two or more places and either seamed or left open on the right side. It was always worn girdled and bloused. In the case of athletes and Amazons (women warriors) it was not pinned on the right shoulder, but allowed to fall free, thus completely baring the right arm.

3. THE FRENCH "BLIAUT" OR "BLIAUD" is a developed tunic which has improved fitting and was an important garment in the Medieval period. There were various neck openings. The sleeves tapered to the wrists, and fair sized gores were added to the side seams, allowing the body of the garment to be narrower and thus more form-fitting. These narrower garments were often laced on the sides, down the back, or down a front opening. As the "bliaut" developed, it became ornamented, decoratively girdled, and ornately sleeved. This diagram shows only the simplest form.

4. THE JERKIN, another version of the tunic, is no doubt one of the handiest little garments in the costumer's collection. It serves for page boys, princes, peasants, and may be worn over tights, puffed trunks, or shorts. Exaggerated shoulder caps may be added for period effect (particularly the sixteenth century), and it may be slightly fitted by darts at the waistline, front and back. Worn over his own blouse and shorts, it transforms Johnny Read into the "Piper's Son." Note: only the composite tunic diagram is drawn to scale.

SHORT TUNICS

GREEK CHITON

BIBLICAL SHEPHERD

CELTIC OR SAXON WARRIOR

MEDIEVAL PAGE

PEASANT

SHORT TUNICS

SHORT GREEK CHITON

The short Greek chiton is here shown as worn by an athlete. The right side may be seamed or left open, since it is held by a girdle. The head opening is formed by pinning the front and back together at either side of the neck. The Greeks used "fibulae," the forerunners of our safety pins, for this purpose. By allowing more fullness in the front of the neck opening, the material falls in soft folds (the cowl neckline). This garment was worn by both men and women. The women's garment was usually ankle length or longer, except in the case of the Amazons mentioned earlier. Sandals may be worn with the chiton, or the actor may be barefoot. There are many variations of the chiton, distinguished by period and purpose; but for all practical purposes this simple form will serve. The long Greek chiton for men is similar in cut but is made floor length plus 2″ to allow for blousing.

SHEPHERD OF BETHLEHEM

For a plain shepherd costume, the tunic (see diagram 1, page 8) with sleeve E may be used. It may have only a neck opening or may be opened down the entire front, banded with contrasting material, and worn lapped and held in place with either a wide or narrow girdle. The simple shepherd costume was often of unbleached wool or coarse linen. Heavy muslin is a good substitute. The nomadic head cloth is worn with it. Sandals and leg strappings are sometimes worn.

CELTIC OR SAXON WARRIOR

This type of costume is representative of many of the warriors during the Dark Ages, with variations of headdress and accessories. Over loosely-fitting breeches, cross-gartered, is worn an undertunic, short-sleeved and usually of soft wool in a rich color: red, dark green, saffron, violet. Over this was often worn a leather jerkin, held in by a wide belt ornamented with metal studs or other heavy decoration. A long cape and some form of helmet are necessary. Soft, shapeless leather shoes were usually tied on. These may be made of cloth (see construction of moccasin in section on Footgear, page 63).

MEDIEVAL PAGE

The jerkin is a good type of tunic for this character, although any short-sleeved, fuller tunic may be used instead. It is most effective when worn over tights or a long-sleeved dance garment (leotard) of contrasting color. Heraldic devices or some other form of ornamentation may be painted on the front or on banding at neck and bottom.

PEASANT

Common to parts of Russia and Central Europe is a development of the tunic with very full lower sleeves added to sleeve B in diagram 1, page 8. A stand-up straight collar or a turned-back one, as shown, was added to the round neck. This shirt was usually of coarse unbleached linen, and the collar, cuffs, and bands on sleeves of red, blue, and yellow embroidery, which for stage purposes may be painted on. The girdle is often red homespun, sometimes an embroidered strip. Any long, bright-colored sash will serve the purpose.

MATERIALS

Since most tunics are a fairly simple form of dress, one finds that they are made of heavy, durable materials. As actually used by the Greeks (chiton) and Egyptians, the tunics were of linen, often so fine as to be transparent. Of course, today we use cotton to simulate the finer fabric. For Biblical shepherds and patriarchs, wool, duvetyn, or some similar coarse drapery material is desirable. Since the Medieval period was one in which very rich fabrics were increasingly popular, a wide range of materials is suggested: cotton, burlap, terry cloth, etc., for peasants; denim, corduroy, and cotton for ordinary tunics; corduroy, velvet, brocades, damask weaves, and other similarly patterned materials for court costumes.

LONG TUNICS

HEBREW

GREEK

MEDIEVAL KING

ANGEL

MEDIEVAL QUEEN

LONG TUNICS

HEBREW

This costume usually consists of an undertunic, long and closed, and an overtunic, slightly longer and open, plus an enormous wrap or shawl (the "aba") thrown over the shoulders. An undertunic and an overtunic which has enormous sleeves are usually enough to create a good effect. The undertunic may be of muslin, either white or light-colored, and the outer tunic should give a rich, warm effect whether it is plain or striped. Drapery materials, old couch covers, or thin striped blankets are fine for this cloaklike garment. Either the headcloth (nomad) or the Near Eastern turbaned fez may be worn with this garment.

LONG GREEK CHITON (Woman's)

The long chiton here illustrated is of the Doric style and has the customary overfold of that garment. An extra length of material is doubled at the top edge for this feature. This fold varies in length from just above the waistline to just below the hips. In the latter case, the overfold is girdled in with the underpart of the blouse, and draped gracefully. The width of material used may be slightly greater than that for the short chiton. It could be the distance from wrist to wrist, arms outstretched, if your fabric is not too heavy and will thus give you a generous amount of material for graceful draping. The material is folded and adjusted by pinning on the shoulders, as described for the short chiton. Variations of headdresses occur. Often only ribbons are used to bind the hair, which is piled high and slightly to the back of the head.

MEDIEVAL KING

The attempt here has been to show a costume suitable for any place and time in the Medieval period, which offers countless variations. It consists of a floor-length, long-sleeved undertunic of good fabric, rich in color and texture; a sleeveless overtunic, contrasting in color, which may be patterned or plain; a long cloak, probably of velveteen, with or without ermine collar; and the usual accessories of jeweled necklace, girdle, crown, mace, etc. The overtunic may be narrower than the one shown, say 30″ in width, which should then be split up the sides for ease in movement.

MEDIEVAL QUEEN

The costume here is based on the "bliaut," with long, full sleeves added just above the elbow. It may include "sleeve-

lets" (extra sleeves of contrasting material caught in the band or held on with an elastic in a casing). This "bliaut" is narrow at the waist and has gores added to the skirt. It is laced at the sides to make it close-fitting.

ANGEL

The very simplest long-sleved tunic with wide neck is appropriate for an angel. Use a thin material such as organdy or thin curtain material. Thin, starched muslin also gives a crisp effect; angels need not droop! Girdle bands and arm bands as well as neck trim are effective in silver or gold ribbon; and the wings (see section on Birds, page 71) may be fastened on by means of a harness of similar or contrasting material. A delicate pattern painted on the body of the costume lends it charm.

OTHER USES FOR BOTH LONG AND SHORT BASIC TUNICS:

MEDIEVAL PEASANT (see illustration on Long Trousers, page 18)

INDIAN (see illustration on Long Trousers, page 18)
Add fringe and decorative yoke to the short tunic with long sleeves.

CHINESE MAN (see illustration on Long Trousers, page 18)
For this simple form of Chinese jacket use the jerkin opened down the front. Add a stand-up collar and use "frogs" or loops to fasten it.

COUNTRY LADS (storybook characters such as Jack the Giant Killer, Peter Piper, and Simple Simon) A simple, loose jerkin over short trousers, and the child's own blouse or T-shirt, with the addition of a quaint hat, is all that is needed to transform a little boy into one of these storybook characters.

JAPANESE KIMONO

This is a tunic which has exceptionally long, pocketlike sleeves added to A. (See diagram 1, page 8.) Seam 1–2 is left open for at least 4″ in each direction. The front opening and neck have a straight continuous piece added which forms a trim and collar in one piece. This piece should be about 2″ wide when finished, and is usually of plain material.

COSTUME FOR CHINESE WOMAN

FRONT

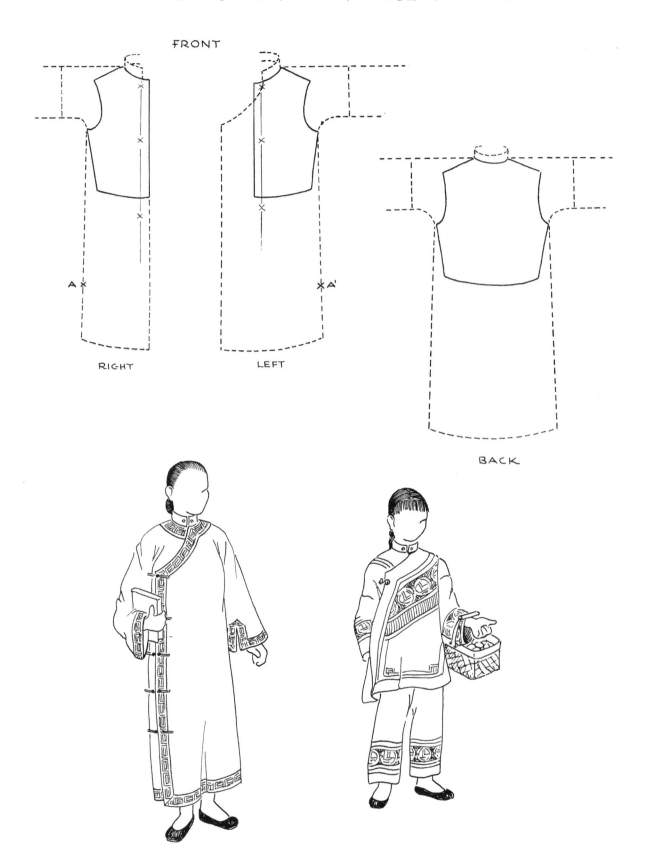

RIGHT

LEFT

BACK

COSTUME FOR CHINESE WOMAN

SINCE the usual costume of the Chinese woman or girl is a peculiar variation of the tunic, it requires individual description. This garment varies in length and may reach to just below the hips, to the knees, or just above the ankles. The shorter types are worn with trousers or a long narrow skirt. The longer tunic becomes a single garment. The cut of the garment is similar for peasant and upper-class Chinese, but the distinction lies in material, embroidery, banding, and fastenings.

In order to ensure proper size for an Occidental figure, it is suggested that the pattern for this tunic be cut in relation to a simple blouse pattern of correct measurements for the wearer. In the accompanying diagram, the ordinary woman's blouse is shown in solid line, the cut of the Chinese gown, in dotted line. The sleeves are cut straight at the shoulder line and are pieced where the width of the material dictates. The right and left fronts are cut differently. The lines designated by three X's mark the center front of each section. A straight stand-up collar about 1½″ deep is fastened to the round neckline, which should be cut to lie close at the base of the throat. This collar may be lined with crinoline or heavy muslin to make it stand up. The curve on the opening, from throat to underarm fastening, varies considerably. It may be a shallow curve which will allow the top clasp to come to the top of the arm's eye, or it may be a diagonal curve which carries to the waistline under the right arm. Since this garment is very narrow and sheathlike, it is usually necessary to leave the side seams open from the bottom to the points marked A and A¹. The back is cut as indicated.

Silk and cotton are the most commonly used materials. Bands contrasting in texture, pattern, and color are used to accent the round neckline, the side opening, and the bottom. These bands are not necessary, especially in the garments of simple people. An outstanding characteristic of all Chinese costumes, however simple, lies in the ingenious fastenings used. These may be buttons and loops, but are more often cleverly twisted or woven "frogs." Most of them serve to suggest a series of horizontal links.

The ornamentation on Chinese costumes is frequently exquisite and delicate embroidery. For stage purposes this can be suggested by painting the bands with tempera or poster paint, with a slight indication of pattern. Although the traditional colors of the Chinese peasant are some kind of greyed blue or black, there is an immense amount of color variation in the costume of the wealthier classes. Color combinations, even those with contrast, are rarely garish. There is great subtlety in the use of small bits of bright color and gold in the ordinary woman's garment. For nobility, there is a wealth of color.

DIAGRAMS--- ALTERATION OF PAJAMA TROUSER PATTERN

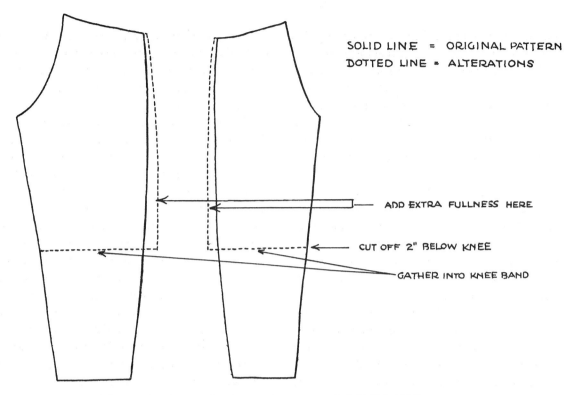

SOLID LINE = ORIGINAL PATTERN
DOTTED LINE = ALTERATIONS

ADD EXTRA FULLNESS HERE

CUT OFF 2" BELOW KNEE

GATHER INTO KNEE BAND

I. DIAGRAM FOR FULL, KNEE-LENGTH BREECHES

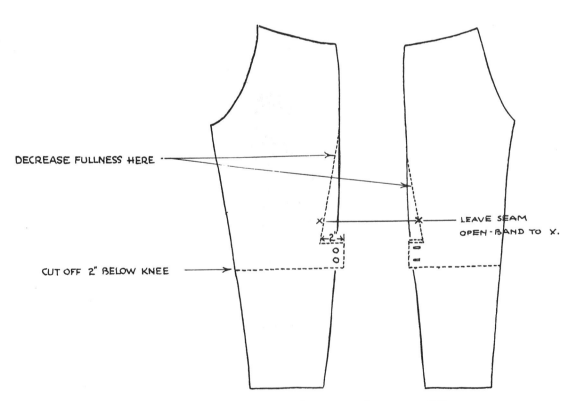

DECREASE FULLNESS HERE

LEAVE SEAM OPEN-BAND TO X.

CUT OFF 2" BELOW KNEE

II. DIAGRAM FOR TIGHT, KNEE-LENGTH BREECHES

TROUSERS

IT IS necessary for the well-stocked costume wardrobe to contain a number of pairs of plain trousers which can be adapted to many purposes. This supply may be made up in part of castoff trousers, shorts, and dungarees, but should include a number of pairs of flannelette, velveteen, denim, sateen, muslin, or other soft but durable materials. These additional trousers should be of several styles: the long, straight trouser; the knee-length, full, knickerbocker-type trouser; and the knee-length, tight trouser. While black and dark blue are substantial colors, they are monotonous if used exclusively, and the wardrobe becomes more flexible if some trousers are of other colors such as rust, golden brown, gold, green, grey blue, and grey. All trousers should be securely fastened, preferably with zippers, and should be held up with belts or suspenders. For trousers worn under tunics, an elastic waistband does the trick but looks rather "bunchy" if worn outside the shirt.

PATTERNS (See illustrations)

Trousers for costumes may be made from any standard man's or woman's pajama pattern or woman's slacks pattern. Since these are always available, the accompanying diagrams show only two possible variations on one of these basic patterns—those for full, knee-length breeches, and those for tight knee-length breeches. (Note descriptions 1 and 2 below.) Shorts patterns are also easy to secure and therefore are not diagrammed.

1. For fairly full knee-length breeches, as worn by Puritan and Dutch colonists, add extra fullness as shown by dotted line, not more than 1½" to 2". Cut 2" below the knee and gather into a band. This may button or tie, depending on the costume.

2. The knee-length, tight-fitting trouser, as worn by several of the European peasants as well as Revolutionary gentlemen, is fitted by taking in the side seam as shown in the illustration, and cutting a flap for buttoning just below the knee. This flap should be reinforced with a lining, the seam left open 2" or 3", and finished as a placket.

3. For long, very full trousers such as are worn by the Dutch and the Turks, extra fullness may be added to the waistline and carried down (as in diagram I) to the ankle. This extra fullness of the waist is disposed of by pleats into a band, in the case of the Dutch, and gathered into the band for Turks, since materials for these are usually light in weight. The Turkish trousers are also gathered in at the ankle. Dutch trousers are sometimes gathered slightly or tapered in just above the shoes.

4. Long, tight-fitting trousers may be cut from the standard pajama-trouser pattern fitted to the wearer by taking in both outside and inside seams. These should come well over the instep in length, as often they are held under the arch of the foot by an elastic band.

5. You may be able to find a costume pattern for a Domino to use for clowns, Pierrot, etc.

6. For most military uniforms it is advisable to try renting costumes, since they can be secured more reasonably than the cost of material and labor in construction.

LONG TROUSERS

TOY SOLDIER

MEDIEVAL PEASANT

SPANISH DANCER

INDIAN

CHINESE

FRONTIERSMAN

LONG TROUSERS

THE ILLUSTRATIONS of long, straight trousers (see opposite page) are all based on a standard man's or woman's pajama or slacks pattern.

TOY SOLDIER

Use the pattern as it comes and add a strip of gold or colored braid down the side seams.

MEDIEVAL PEASANT

Straight trousers made of flannelette or similar soft fabric, unevenly dyed, suggest the rudeness of this costume. The trousers are usually worn cross-gartered or merely wrapped with strips of contrasting material. A soft, loose tunic is worn over the trousers, sometimes turned up on one side and tucked into the belt. Soft, shapeless shoes complete the costume.

SPANISH DANCER

These trousers are best made of black velveteen or heavy black sateen. Narrow the trousers for a closer fit through the thighs and knees by taking in both inside and outside seams. Pin this alteration to suit the individual actor, and be sure to allow enough room for easy movement. For the flare at the bottom, open up the outside seam about 9" and insert a godet. This may be of the same material as the trousers—as would be the case in a sailor's trousers; or, as in the case of the Spanish trousers, the godet may be of a silky fabric of a bright color. This inset in the dance costume is usually knife-pleated. In the Spanish costume there are usually two or three metal buttons running up the seam above the godet.

PIONEER (Frontiersman)

He wears straight trousers of a heavy material, or dungarees tucked into boots.

INDIAN

This illustration does not attempt to depict the costume of any one tribe but simply suggests "Indian." It is fairly typical of the costume worn by the Plains Indians. Trousers made of khaki or light brown flannelette should have fringes up the side seams. These fringes were in many cases the tails of small animals. Knotted cloth makes a good substitute for this.

CHINESE

Trousers are worn by both men and women in China and may be straight or cuffed according to usage and weather. Often the straight trousers are banded at the bottom with a piece of contrasting material about 1½" wide. Sometimes there is a short split up the side, with banding following the opening. For winter wear the clothes of the Chinese are often padded and quilted. Trousers of this heavy sort are drawn in at the ankle. Sometimes several layers of these garments are worn, creating a very "stuffed" appearance.

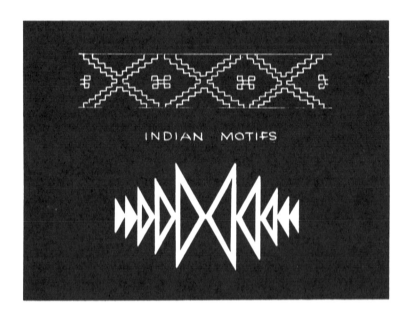

INDIAN MOTIFS

SHORT TROUSERS

PURITAN

DANISH PEASANT

PIXIE

DWARF

BAVARIAN

[20]

SHORT TROUSERS

THE TROUSERS on the opposite page, with the exception of the short, straight ones, can be developed from the pajama-trouser pattern according to diagrams I and II, page 16. The Bavarian pants and the Pixie shorts can be made from boys' shorts or pants patterns put out by commercial pattern companies.

PURITAN

Trousers for this costume are of the full knee-length type shown in diagram I. Those worn by the Dutch colonists were similar but slightly fuller, and an inch or so longer to provide more blouse over the knee band. Quakers and the Southern colonists also wore this type of trouser. The tunic or jacket can be developed from the pajama-jacket pattern. Directions for constructing the hat are given in the section on Hats. Materials should be plain, suggesting wool, and can be of any dull, dark colors: grey, rust, black, greyed green, or blue.

DANISH PEASANT

While this illustration was drawn from a Danish costume, it is equally typical of other Scandinavian costumes and many of the Central European breeches. The trousers are made from the pajama-trouser pattern, with the alterations suggested in diagram II, page 16. The Scandinavian trousers were often fastened at the top by means of a wide cloth belt attached to the breeches and buttoned in center front. This may be suggested by making an extra cloth belt to be worn over the trousers. Knitted garter bands with wool tasseled ends were frequently worn over the knee bands.

BAVARIAN

This type of short straight trouser is worn by many men of the Alpine regions. They are always of sturdy fabric and often very bright in color, with rich yarn embroidery to accent seams and pockets. The trousers are held up by means of ornamental suspenders of felt or leather. A wide leather belt is a usual addition to the costume.

PIXIE

Ordinary shorts with a cotton jersey shirt and some sort of round or peaked hat are usually enough to suggest this fanciful figure. Bright woods colors and amusing patterns on the shirt or hat will remove the figure from the realm of everyday play clothes.

DWARF

Tight knee breeches and jerkin or vest, slightly exaggerated to shorten the appearance of the figure, and a fantastic cap, are enough to suggest the Dwarf.

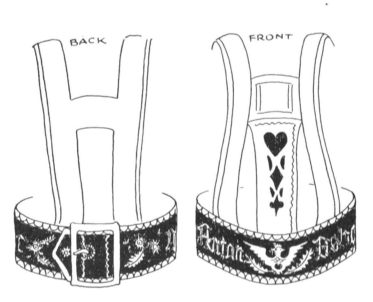

BAVARIAN BELT AND BRACES

VEST DIAGRAMS

DOTTED LINE = ALTERATIONS

SCALE - $\frac{1}{8}'' = 1''$

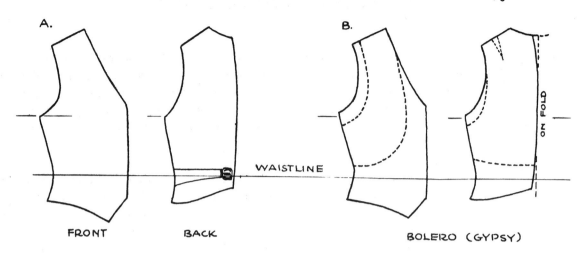

A.

WAISTLINE

FRONT   BACK

B.

ON FOLD

BOLERO (GYPSY)

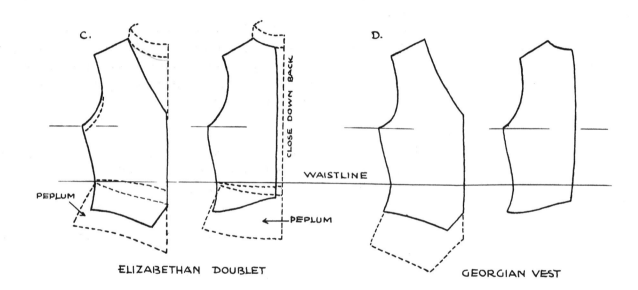

C.

CLOSE DOWN BACK

PEPLUM

PEPLUM

ELIZABETHAN DOUBLET

D.

WAISTLINE

GEORGIAN VEST

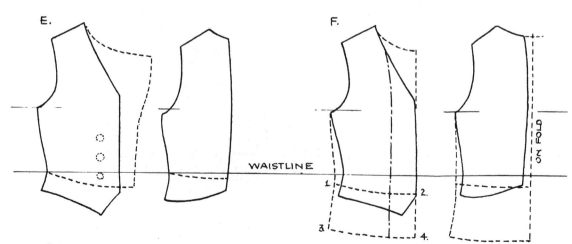

E.

WAISTLINE

DOUBLE-BREASTED VEST
WITH REVERS

F.

1.   2.

3.   4.

ON FOLD

CZECH., PIRATE AND POLISH BOLERO
JACKETS

VEST DIAGRAMS

MANY variations can be made on the man's vest pattern to meet the needs of both short jackets and vests. A few typical patterns are here offered. A commercial pattern for either a man's or a woman's vest may be bought, or a pattern can be made from a simple vest you have on hand.

The solid line in the accompanying diagrams shows a typical man's vest of a small size. The dotted lines indicate alterations necessary for type or period. Since these diagrams are drawn to scale as indicated, you can figure the approximate measurements for changes. These will vary considerably with different figures, but will suffice to plot general adjustments. Diagram A is the ordinary vest used as a basic pattern for all the variations here shown.

BOLERO (diagram B)

This type of bolero, shown in illustration of Gypsy, page 26, is worn by both men and women, and may be based on a woman's blouse pattern as well as on the vest. The shoulder seams should be narrowed and the armhole enlarged in all cases.

ELIZABETHAN DOUBLET (diagram C)

The doublet may be opened either in front or back; but since the front is usually rather richly ornamented and frequently requires padding, the back opening often proves to be more practical. A zipper is the ideal fastening for this garment. Extend the center front line to the base of the neck. Enlarge the armhole a trifle to accommodate the usual padding or ornamental roll. Shape the waistline to a slight point in center front, and cut a peplum, as shown, to flare slightly over the full slashed breeches. A straight collar band should be added, to which the ruff may be attached if one is desired. Sleeves may be attached to the doublet or to an undergarment.

COLONIAL VEST (diagram D)

The waistcoat of the Colonial period was considerably longer than in many other times, and the point was exaggerated both in length and in its slant toward the sides. The back of this vest is normal.

DOUBLE-BREASTED VEST (diagram E)

This vest has rather exaggerated revers, which are cut as shown in relation to the widened front. (See illustration for Vest of 1805, page 24.) Buttons show where the double-breasted vest will fasten.

COMPOSITE DIAGRAM FOR LONG AND SHORT STRAIGHT JACKETS

Simple jackets such as those illustrated for the Pirate, Czechoslovakian, and Polish peasants are easily plotted from a basic vest pattern. Cut the neck high for Pirate and Czechoslovakian. Cut on the dot-dash line for front of the longer Polish jacket. Shorten on line 1-2 for the Czech and Pirate jacket. Extend the garment to line 3-4 for the Polish jacket. Since it is often faced on the right side (with contrasting color), no hem allowance need be considered.

VESTS

ELIZABETHAN
DOUBLET

GEORGIAN

1805

1830

1860

1870

1890

VESTS

THE VEST is a versatile little garment, and even a small collection of them can help you in numerous ways. It is possible to put new faces on some of them to create various period and humorous effects. They will undergo a surprising amount of refashioning. The vest is a simple garment to make, and with one basic pattern and some good pictures of period or national styles you can quite easily create any style you may want. All vests should be made of strong, durable materials, since they are fitted tightly and are often subjected to considerable strain. They should be made double, especially in the front. The backs may be treated more casually, since many of those are never seen. Some kind of belt or tape should be attached at underarm seams to help fit the back snugly and hold the garment in place.

ELIZABETHAN DOUBLET

The doublet may be considered either as a vest or a jacket, but since it can be drafted on a vest pattern, it is placed here. It should be of rather luxurious fabric and should be lined and even padded slightly in the front to give a stiff effect. It can be made over a crinoline lining with a layer of quilt padding between it and the outside fabric. The peplum should be lined with crinoline. If sleeves are to be attached to the doublet, cut the armhole according to a shirt or jacket pattern; but since sleeves could be sewn to a roughly made undergarment, the armhole of the vest may be slightly enlarged to carry the extra padded roll so typical of the period.

GEORGIAN (AMERICAN COLONIAL)

Construction of this vest is described in diagram D, page 22, but a word must be said about material. The waistcoats of the wealthy men of the period were extremely elaborate, as were all parts of the costume. The material used should seem to be of silk or satin, light in color, and should be patterned. Flowered prints, damasks, or quilted fabrics are suitable. Gold or silk braid or ornamental binding helps to create a rich effect. False pockets placed rather low on the points of the waistcoat add a great deal to the decorative effect.

OTHER PERIODS

A few vests, typical of the nineteenth century, are illustrated. The short vests accompany the cutaway coat and the Prince Albert. The pointed and double-pointed front cuts were used more extensively in the later part of the period.

BOLERO JACKETS

PIRATE

CZECHOSLOVAKIAN

MEXICAN

GYPSY

BOLERO JACKETS

THE BOLERO is a short jacket, usually without sleeves. It may be cut from a standard vest pattern as indicated on diagram B, page 22. It may also be drafted from a blouse or pajama-shirt pattern; but since it should be rather close-fitting, the vest measurements need less alteration, hence they are used here.

CZECHOSLOVAKIAN JACKET

This short, straight, sleeveless jacket is a part of many Central European peasant costumes. It is very often of heavy wool, quite richly ornamented with embroidery or appliqué in bright colors. Flannelette or drapery fabrics make excellent substitutions for wool, and the ornamentation may be suggested with tempera paint or rough appliqué. The blouse, hat, and fringed trousers are distinctly Czechoslovakian.

PIRATE BOLERO

The pirate bolero is cut almost exactly like the jacket described above, except that originally it provided for buttoning. Since these jackets were worn most casually, they do not actually have to button, and the fastening may be simulated rather than functional. Dark colors and brass buttons are the usual order. A loose shirt, loose flowing trousers (which may be longer than shown and tucked into boots), head scarf, neckerchief, and long flowing sash of brilliant color, complete the costume. The typical pirate captain's costume is some variation of eighteenth century costume: a tricorn hat (sometimes on top of the head scarf), long dark "colonial" coat (heavily braided and brass buttoned), cuffed boots, or buckled shoes.

GYPSY BOLERO

The small, curved bolero so commonly thought of as "gypsy" is typically Spanish. It may be of any bright color and fabric and is more effective if it is fairly plain, trimmed only by means of binding, or a few sequins or coins sewn on the edges. It will then be a little island of strong contrast in a composition of gaily patterned and brilliantly colored skirt, blouse, sash, and scarf.

MEXICAN JACKET

This form of the bolero is purely Spanish and is worn by Mexicans of the upper classes, particularly the wealthy ranchers. It has become a popular form of festive dress. The jacket must be of very strong material, suggesting the texture of heavy wool or felt, as it must be fitted snugly. Sleeves and armholes may be cut from any jacket pattern. The trimming of this costume is usually elaborate braiding and embroidery.

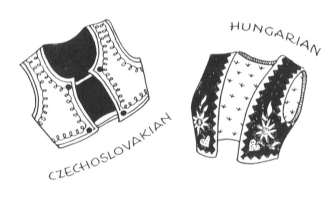

JACKET DIAGRAMS
SCALE - ⅛" = 1"

MAN'S PAJAMA BLOUSE

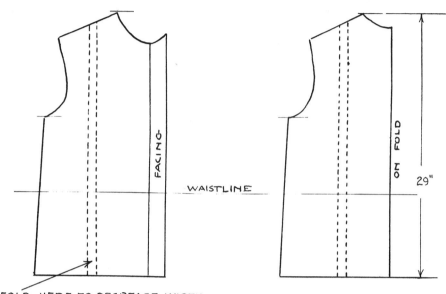

FACING

WAISTLINE

ON FOLD

29"

FOLD HERE TO DECREASE WIDTH

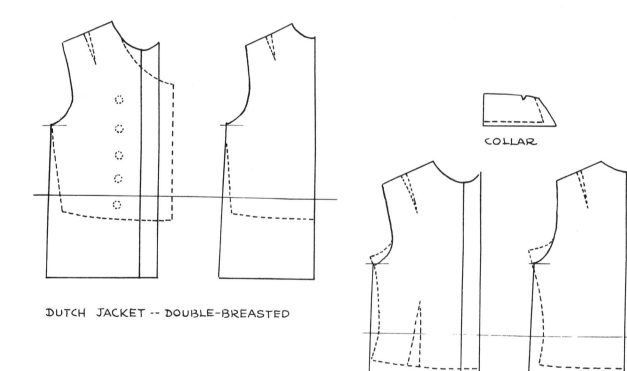

DUTCH JACKET -- DOUBLE-BREASTED

COLLAR

TYROLEAN - FITTED

JACKET DIAGRAMS

For ORDINARY jackets there are many standard patterns, both men's and women's, and there are usually sports jackets of all sorts which may be borrowed or which have been donated to your costume collection. These, if you own them, may be altered and decorated to suggest period and national styles. Many times, however, you will need to create little coats or jackets of a particular type. To meet this need, one or two examples of how to change the ordinary man's or boy's pajama-shirt pattern may prove helpful. As it is, the pajama shirt is usually quite wide on the shoulders, and it is recommended that at least 1″ of the width be taken out of the pattern by folding as shown on the dotted lines. These diagrams are drawn to scale so that you can use them as a guide in drafting your own pattern for such a shirt.

DUTCH JACKET

The solid line indicates the pajama-shirt pattern with an inch taken out of the width. The Dutch jacket is short, double-breasted, and rather close-fitting under the arms. Therefore, the alteration for front sections is shown by the dotted lines. This includes underarm fitting, darts on the shoulders, and extension of the section to provide for overlapping. The buttons indicate the amount of this lap.

TYROLEAN FITTED JACKET

For the short, snugly-fitted jacket common to many of the mountainous regions of Europe, use the pajama-shirt pattern as shown in heavy line, and include the collar. The length should be 3″- 4″ below the waistline. The underarm alteration will take care of part of the fitting, and darts in the front sections will further assist this. Darts on the shoulder must be taken both front and back. Since most pajama collars are designed with rather long points, these must be decreased and the collar narrowed as shown. The armholes should be cut slightly smaller and a corresponding amount taken out of the underarm seam of the sleeve.

JACKETS

DUTCH

TYROLEAN

POLISH

1800

JACKETS

DUTCH JACKET

The cut of this jacket is suggested under Jacket diagrams, page 28. It should look bulky but tight-fitting. Therefore, rather thick materials are best to use: drapery fabrics, denim, flannelette (doubled), or quilted materials. It is made to button tightly across the chest and even seems to create horizontal wrinkles. It is usually collarless and worn with a neck scarf. Contrary to general impression, these jackets are not always of blue or greyed colors but are sometimes rich, warm colors such as pink, orange, and gold, which contrast strikingly with the dark, full trousers.

TYROLEAN JACKET

While a method for cutting this small coat jacket from a pajama shirt is diagrammed, any standard fitted-jacket pattern will serve. The only necessities are that it be short and close-fitting in waist and sleeves. The material should suggest wool, and popular colors are dark green with red trim, red with green trim, golden brown with green or black trim. Metal buttons, braid binding, and simple ornamental stitching are used for trim. The wide leather belt, very heavily embossed or studded, is particularly Tyrolean.

POLISH SLEEVELESS COAT

Particularly Slavic is this straight, sleeveless jacket of the Pole. It is generally of extremely thick wool, almost like felt, very straight in cut, with wide shoulders, and is quite richly ornamented with embroidery. Sometimes the real jacket is lined with fur, and the edging here suggested as fringe is a band of coarse fur. Many of these jackets are of a natural wool color, a beautiful background for brilliant decoration; some are black, with much white in the decoration; some are of brilliant golds and reds. The leg wrappings usually repeat the color scheme of the jacket. They are simply strips of wool, long enough to wrap around the leg at least twice, and have curved ends which carry an ornamental bit of embroidery.

BOY OF 1800

This short coat, the forerunner of the Eton jacket, can be made from a boy's blouse or pajama-shirt pattern by decreasing the width as shown on Jacket diagrams, page 28, and narrowing the sleeves. Any girl's round collar pattern may be used. Ruffles on the collar and at cuffs of sleeves are important to suggest the so-called Romantic period.

POLISH LEG WRAPPING

DIAGRAMS FOR ACCESSORIES TO THE BODICE DRESS

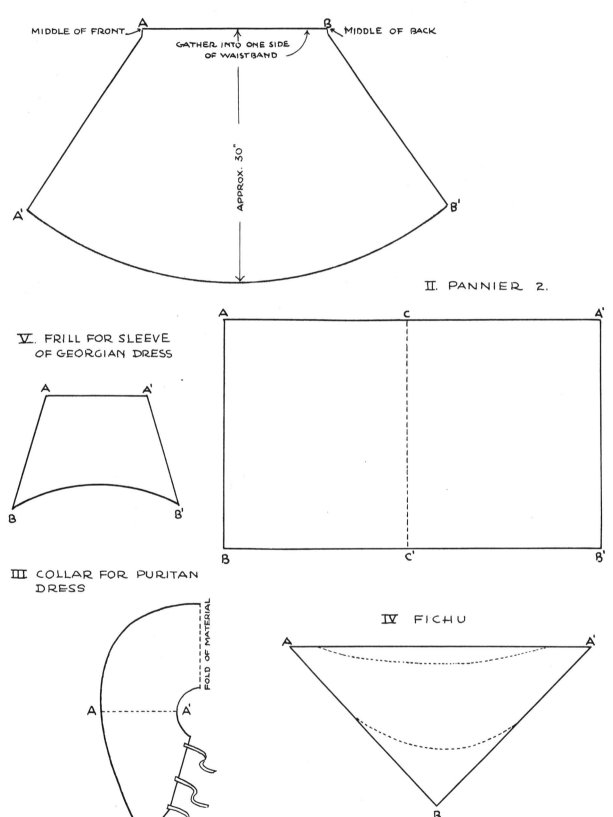

I. PANNIER 1.

MIDDLE OF FRONT → A B ← MIDDLE OF BACK

GATHER INTO ONE SIDE
OF WAISTBAND

APPROX. 30"

A' B'

II. PANNIER 2.

A C A'

B C' B'

V. FRILL FOR SLEEVE
OF GEORGIAN DRESS

A A'

B B'

III COLLAR FOR PURITAN
DRESS

FOLD OF MATERIAL

A A'

IV FICHU

A A'

B

ACCESSORIES TO THE BODICE DRESS

One of the basic costumes in any collection is the simple bodice dress. Succeeding pages suggest several uses for it. This dress may be made from any bodice dress pattern available. Under *Special Costumes* such as Colonial Woman, pattern companies often include variations such as several sleeves, panniers, fichus and collars. However, changes in the basic dress are easy for the person with average sewing ability.

ACCESSORIES TO THE BODICE DRESS

Panniers may be made by either of two methods. In diagram 1 for a graceful pannier, cut material roughly in the shape indicated, allowing one and one half times the measurement from center front to center back for A-B, and about 30″ for depth. Gather A-A¹ and B-B¹ and fasten to centers front and back. If a ruffle is desired, it is sewn on line A¹-B¹.

Diagram II shows a pannier made of a straight piece of material. A-A¹ should be at least twice the waist measurement and is gathered into the waistband. A-B and A¹-B¹ are gathered up and fastened at either side of center front. C-C¹ is gathered to about 10″ and fastened center back. This makes a bulkier pannier than diagram I and carries the fullness around the back.

Diagram III shows the shape of collar used for a Puritan costume. A-A¹ should be at least 3″ more than the shoulder width. This collar is best made double, of fine material, starched. It should tie in two or three places down the front.

A fichu (diagram IV) may be made of a simple triangle in which A-A¹ is the diagonal of a 36″ square. A more graceful fichu is achieved if the point B is rounded off as shown by dotted line in the diagram, and if A-A¹ is also slightly curved. A ruffle is added to line A-B-A¹.

In diagram V a frill of lace for sleeve of colonial costume is cut in shape as indicated. A-A¹ is at least one and one half times the arm measurement at point of attachment. Make a seam by joining A-B and A¹-B¹.

BODICE DRESS

TYROLEAN

AMERICAN PIONEER

DUTCH (MIDDLEBURG)

ROMANTIC   1820 - 40

BODICE DRESS

AMERICAN PIONEER

The pioneer dress in illustration shows the bodice dress in its simplest form. It should be made of simple cotton, plain or figured, or of some material suggesting homespun. The sleeves are long, in this case, and merely rolled back. They should be plain, whether long or short, and may be cuffed to match the collar. It is not necessary to add the peplum, but it does give added interest of line to a plain garment.

TYROLEAN PEASANT

Many peasant dresses are of the bodice-dress type, although in most provinces one finds the blouse-bodice-skirt combination more usual. This illustration is typical of Salzburg and is meant to represent a type rather than an actual reproduction. Small, gaily colored cotton print is a good material to use. Trim, such as guimpe, ruffles, button band, etc., may be white, but is rather more interesting in vigorous color. A long apron of white or color may be used with this costume.

DUTCH

One of the typical Dutch costumes is this from Middleburg. A low-cut, laced bodice waist is worn over a finely gathered white guimpe. Sleeves are short and very tight. In this section of Holland, strings of coral are worn around the neck, collar fashion. A dark apron nearly matching the dress in color is worn, as well as a small, close-fitting cap.

ROMANTIC PERIOD (1820-1840)

This dress is a variation of the plain bodice dress. The waist is extremely high (just below the breasts) and the skirt is somewhat less full, often being slightly gored to dispose of some of the fullness at the waistline. The neckline should be low and may be either round or square. A peasant-blouse pattern may be used for the waist instead of the regular bodice-dress pattern, as it was often quite full and had short, puffed sleeves. Since this was a period of daintiness, the material should be light in weight and delicate in color. Flowered fabrics were popular, and the dresses were trimmed with ribbons, ruffles, pleating, and flowers.

BODICE DRESS

GEORGIAN

BALLET DANCER

PURITAN

1860

BODICE DRESS

(Continued)

GEORGIAN (AMERICAN COLONIAL)

The straight bodice dress forms the foundation for this costume. The waist should be opened down the front with zipper or hooks. This seam line is sometimes decorated with small bows. The skirt may be slashed down the front, and an inset (slightly triangular) put in. This is effective if it is quite in contrast to the rest of the costume in color and is richly flowered or quilted. Long, lace ruffles on the sleeves and a lace or ruffled fichu are necessary. Panniers are described on the diagram sheet of this section. Several crinoline petticoats or hoops should be worn. Panniers of crinoline may be worn under this dress to build out the hips.

BALLET DRESS

This is a costume used not only for dance but for several types of circus performers. The bodice should be cut low in the front and opened down the back. Since it must be fitted tightly, the bodice must be made of strong material: muslin, sateen or percale. It is advisable to make it double and to reinforce it with boning in center front, center back and along vertical dart lines in front and back.

The skirt should be made of nylon net and ought to have four or five layers of material. Each layer should carry as much fullness as you can work into the waist band. Nylon net is 72″ wide. Try to use at least one width for each layer. The length is generally measured from the waistline to 5″ above the knee. Short panties edged with a ruffle are worn with this ballet skirt, so allow extra material for this and any other trim you may want to include. Try various colors of net, one over the other for color change.

1860

This illustration is of the plainest type of Mid-Victorian dress. The drop shoulder and bell-shaped sleeves were typical of the period. The sleevelet of white worn under the wide sleeve is simply made as full cylinder, banded at the wrist, and held to the arm just above the elbow by an elastic in a casing at that end of the cylinder. The skirt should be extremely full (about 5 yards) to allow for hoops or several crinoline petticoats to be worn underneath. The more elegant dresses of the period were very elaborate indeed, and were richly trimmed with bows and garlands of ribbons and lace or artificial flowers. One should consult books of period costume, or plates such as those from *Godey's Ladies' Book*, for suggestions of the rich variations of this period.

PURITAN

This dress is exactly like the pioneer dress except for the addition of the long cape collar and deep cuffs. The collar is diagrammed on page 32. The apron is not necessary for outdoor wear but is often used, as it repeats the light note of collars, cuffs, and bonnet facing. Dark, quiet colors should be used for this costume. Sateen and flannel are excellent materials.

NOTE:

Additional characters for whom the bodice dress is a good foundation are: Mother Goose, witches, Quakers, servants of the Victorian period, and country women (periodless).

DIAGRAMS FOR BODICES

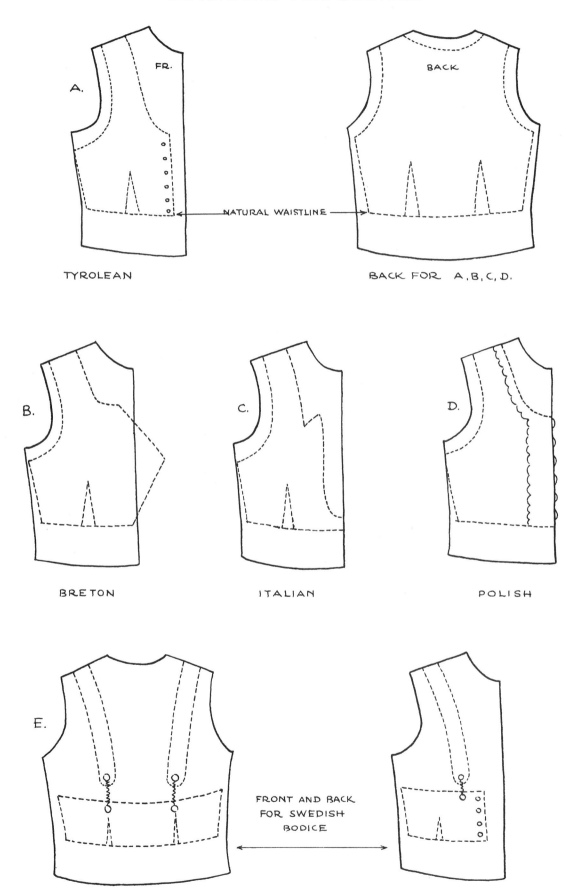

A.

FR.

BACK

NATURAL WAISTLINE

TYROLEAN

BACK FOR A, B, C, D.

B.

BRETON

C.

ITALIAN

D.

POLISH

E.

FRONT AND BACK
FOR SWEDISH
BODICE

BODICES

THERE are as many types of bodices as there are provinces in the European countries. In many sections of Europe, especially in the Tyrol, France, and Sweden, there are certain cuts of this garment, which, with headdress and apron, not only distinguish the inhabitants of a particular town but also identify the married and single women. It is impossible and unnecessary for the average costumer to do the amount of research needed for an accurate presentation of these distinctive differences. Since the plain bodice, low-cut and laced in the front (such as the Tyrolean bodice illustrated on page 40), is suggestive of many countries, it is practical to have a few of these in dark colors, of durable materials, and with strong linings, in the wardrobe for general use. These may be given a certain amount of novelty by adding decorative details, such as embroidery or appliquéd flowers, or by changing the colors of the lacings, perhaps substituting a chain and silver ornaments for the more usual ribbons or tapes. Let it be said in passing that any bodice lasts as long as its fastening. Therefore, be sure that the front openings are reinforced with strong muslin, and the eyelets and buttonholes firmly made. It is possible on strong materials to use metal eyelets inserted by means of an eyelet punch. These may be secured from any craft-supply house where materials for leather work are carried.

Bodices vary in type from those resembling an exaggerated belt, with suspenders, to some almost indistinguishable from a jacket. All may be cut from an ordinary woman's blouse pattern without yoke. The wide belt type must be fitted by means of darts front and back rather than cut as a belt, since it must closely follow the body curves.

The accompanying diagram shows how a few varying bodices may be designed by altering the ordinary blouse pattern. In all cases the underarm seam must be taken in, the armhole enlarged, and shoulder seam narrowed as shown. Darts should be taken in both front and back sections for the closely-fitted bodice. Measurements cannot be given for these alterations and darts, as they must be made to adjust to individual figures. The regular blouse pattern allows for overlapping of front sections. Hence, these diagrams are planned around the center front line.

The Russian or Polish bodice is more loosely-fitted, and the darts may be omitted if any excess fullness is removed. All bodices should be lined, since the tight fitting causes considerable strain on them. Buttons with loops, or zipper, may be used as fastenings where eyelets and lacing are not necessary for the effect.

BODICES AND BLOUSES

SWEDISH

ITALIAN

TYROLEAN

MEXICAN

BODICES AND BLOUSES

SINCE the bodice is never worn without a blouse, it is necessary to consider the blouse as carefully as the bodice itself if an accurate national suggestion is desired. Three or four general types of blouses are used: the short, puffed-sleeve blouse with low neck; the long, full-sleeved blouse with high round neck; the simple, long-sleeved, collared shirtwaist type, and the heavily embroidered, drop-shouldered, tunic-type blouse worn by the Poles, Russians, and other Eastern European women. The illustrations here attempt to show the typical blouse worn with various kinds of bodices.

ITALIAN

While this bodice is typical of those worn in certain parts of southern Italy, it is strangely like one found in a particular section of Norway. In itself it is an interesting enough variant from the usual to be included merely for the pleasure of its design. In the Italian version, the bodice is of two colors, dull red and dull blue, with black- and gold-thread embroidery. Since this bodice is fastened only at the waist-line, the "wings" of the front sections should be lined with crinoline or other stiff material. The blouse is of coarse, rather than transparent, cotton and of ordinary cut.

SWEDISH

The wide-belt type bodice is only one of many charming patterns from this locality. The clasps of both bodice and suspenders in many Scandinavian countries are of silver, and the bodices are sometimes laced with silver chains tipped with bell-shaped ornaments. In both Sweden and Norway a simple cotton blouse with collar is usually worn with all bodices. These blouses are often ornamented with hemstitching or simple embroidery in red and white.

TYROLEAN

The bodice here illustrated is one of the simplest and most usual of all the bodices. It is a narrowly cut garment which features the lacing. Ribbons of several colors are often used to lend variation to a group. The trim may be bands of contrasting plain color, or may be embroidered (suggested by painting pattern on the material). While a short puffed-sleeve blouse may be worn, the one here shown with collar and ruffled sleeve offers a charming contrast to the severity of the bodice.

MEXICAN

This illustration is included principally for the blouse, which is of very fine cotton with a deep embroidered ruffle around a low neck. There are many blouse patterns available for this garment. The scarf is a usual accompaniment to this blouse; and since it is long, it is worn wrapped around the waist, and worn over the shoulders, with the ends tucked into the waistband. This often creates the effect of a suspender-type bodice.

APRONS

ITALIAN

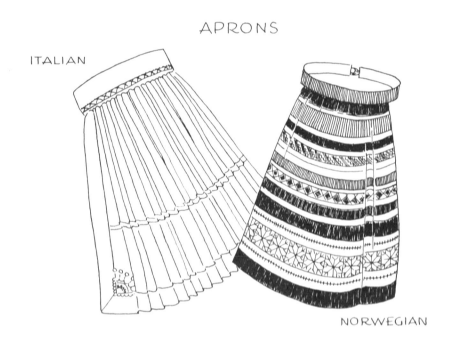

NORWEGIAN

BODICES AND BLOUSES

POLISH OR
RUSSIAN

POLISH OR
RUSSIAN

BRETON

BRETON

[42]

BODICES AND BLOUSES

(A Few National Variations)

POLISH OR RUSSIAN

Typical of Poland, some parts of Russia, and other Eastern European countries is this rather loosely-fitted, jacket-like bodice which is worn either open or closed. It is usually of black or another very dark color, and is ornamented with light bandings, patterns of buttons, or maybe embroidered in white and other light colors. A typical Polish or Russian blouse is here shown. This is traditionally made of coarse linen with very full raglan sleeves. Wide bands of colored embroidery ornament the sleeves and neck openings. This embroidery often is done in red and black, red and blue, or black and white. The effect of much embroidery on both blouse and bodice is effective on the stage.

The tunic blouse for the man is included to round out the scheme, since costumes of this sort are usual for folk dances. The color and pattern in the embroidery, for both men and women, will create a good balance and unity in the ensemble.

BRETON (French)

There are many delightful French variations of the bodice, but those of the Bretons are so interestingly cut and ornamented that at least one of them seemed irresistible. Extremely wide bands of decoration make this and similar Breton bodices seem very heavy and rich, which indeed they are, especially in contrast to the fine lace or delicate, starched cotton of the Breton cap.

The French fisherman's smock is here shown because it offers a suggestion for using simple smocks which are easily secured. Many peasant farmers and craftsmen in the Tyrol as well as in many parts of France wear similar short smocks. It was also a favorite garment with farmers and the simple tradespeople of England during the eighteenth and early nineteenth centuries. The French smock is by tradition a soft blue of medium value, and is worn over dark trousers. The soft black French beret is the natural accompaniment to this costume.

THE STRAIGHT SKIRT

IRISH

BRETON CHILD

POLISH

SWISS

MEXICAN

[44]

THE STRAIGHT SKIRT

IT TAKES little imagination to realize the importance of having in any costume collection a number of simple skirts, long and short, sober and gay, plain or patterned. Three types of skirt will prove valuable: the straight, gathered skirt, the gored skirt, and the circular. Of these, the straight, full skirt is the most universal and versatile. In planning all skirts, try to think of them as several-purpose garments, and plan waistbands that can be adjusted in size several inches, hems which can be turned up or let down, and seams sufficiently deep to admit of alteration. Think of materials durable enough to stand up under repeated dyeing and revamping.

The full, straight skirt is a basic part of many dresses, as one can see by glancing through this or any other costume book. The bodice dress of pioneer or peasant, the colonial and crinoline lady, the gypsy, the bareback rider, the ballet dancer, all call for skirts of this type. Practically any peasant European, Latin American, or just plain country woman without nationality is suitably dressed in straight skirt, with or without apron. A simple blouse, bodice, and head-dress or kerchief are the usual companions to this skirt.

It is not necessary to diagram the construction of this garment, for from our earliest days of dressing dolls we have solved its problems. But some suggestion of materials and decorative treatment for the stage might prove practical. Any firm cotton material is good for simple skirts. Unbleached muslin, sateen, percale, chintzes, and light-weight drapery fabrics all make inexpensive and practical skirts. Flannelette, if not too heavy, is good for skirts when you want to suggest wool. Petticoats of coarse cotton help to give these skirts the bulky character they usually need, but making them very full is quite necessary. Use three widths of 36″ material as a minimum, and four or five if the material is soft and you want a voluminous garment. If striped and figured material is not available, you can spray or paint plain muslin to get the effect you desire. (See directions in section on Dyeing and Surface Treatment of Fabrics, page 4.)

IRISH PEASANT

This figure is suggestive of all peasant types (except the Welsh) in the British Isles, both past and present. Irish and Scotch fisherwomen, particularly, wear this kind of costume. It consists of a long, straight skirt, usually plain and dark, a dark blouse, a checked or finely striped apron, and a fringed shawl worn over the head or on the shoulders. Many French peasants wear a similar dress for everyday use, re-serving the distinctive provincial costume for festive occasions. The shawls vary in size and often are worn crossed over the breast and tied at the back or tucked into the skirt band, as shown in the illustration of the French child.

POLISH PEASANT

A characteristic of several types of Polish peasant skirt is the extensive use of rich vertical stripes. The illustration is of a very festive dress for which the material is a stiff, closely woven wool. Both the skirt and its apron are patterned in wide stripes, strong in color and value contrast. A close-fitting bodice and the usual embroidered linen blouse is worn with this skirt.

SWISS PEASANT

Peasant dress in many parts of the Alpine region resembles this somewhat composite illustration. Material for this skirt may be of almost any color, but a great deal of rich blue, red, or black was used. It may be plain or patterned with small figures. The bodice may be plain and made of black, red, green, or blue. A simple, long-sleeved, full, muslin blouse is worn under the bodice. The neckerchief may be worn as shown, tied as a fichu, or discarded altogether.

MEXICAN

A long, very full cotton skirt of either light or dark material is used for this costume. Colors vary, and for the stage much richer colors than are usually worn may be emphasized for theatrical effect. The skirt may be plain or edged with a deep ruffle or flounce as shown. A loose cotton blouse is worn over the skirt, and the distinguishing feature, the dark rebosa, is wrapped around the shoulders and head. The long scarf has many functional uses in addition to being a head covering. It binds infants and other burdens to the back of the Mexican woman. It often forms a sling to assist in holding the load which a peasant woman often carries in her arms. The rebosa is usually dark blue and black.

GORED SKIRT

Several patterns for the gored skirt will be of use to the costumer for securing some period effects and for contemporary costume. Since its use was principally at the end of the nineteenth century and the beginning of the twentieth, the need for it in general costuming is not very great. All commercial-pattern companies carry patterns for four-, six-, and eight-gore skirts. Occasionally one can secure an old pattern of the periods mentioned.

DIAGRAM – SEMICIRCULAR SKIRT
SCALE – $\frac{1}{16}$" = 1"

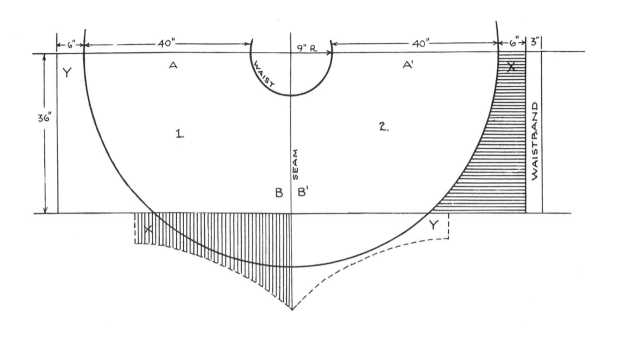

SEMICIRCULAR SKIRT

THE SEMICIRCULAR skirt is an important item in the costumer's collection, for it can serve for a cape as well as a skirt. While patterns are nearly always available for this garment because of the recurrence of style interest in this particular cut, it is convenient to know how to plot your own pattern for the simplest form of the circular skirt. A diagram drawn to scale (as indicated) is here offered. This diagram is planned for the ordinary 36" material without nap. The problem is very much simpler if wider material can be used. The amount of 36" material neded for a semi-circular skirt depends, of course, on the length required and the size of the waist opening. This diagram is planned for a 40" length and a 27" waistband. It calls for 3¼ yards of materials.

First cut 3" off for the waistband and mark the center of the remaining material. Using an appropriate radius to secure a waist opening, describe a half circle at center fold. Remember the formula (circumference = diameter x 3.14) and secure your radius measurement by working from your waist measure. Using the same center as in describing the waist opening and the length of the skirt desired, plus the radius of waist as the new radius, draw the outer circle as shown. Since 36" material will not accommodate the entire curve, it will have to be pieced. Cut down center fold and piece section Y to section 2, and section X to section 1. Seam B and B¹ after piecing and cutting. Seam A and A¹ within 6" of waist to form placket. This seam (A and A¹) may be left open for capes and for dance skirts where a side opening is desired.

COATS AND CLOAKS

THE PROBLEM of the coat is one to shake the stoutest heart. There is no simple path to its solution. Since its emergence from the various capes or mantˡes and cloaks in the latter part of the Renaissance Period, and its rather sudden development into a highly complicated garment, it has become a major consideration to the costumer. Coats as we know them require such expert cutting, fitting, padding, and such firm materials that, for the average costumer, it is more practical and far cheaper to rent or borrow them than to make them. So far as the coat is casual, resembling a developed jacket or tunic, or insofar as it seems to be a sleeved cape, there is no reason to avoid its construction. Such coats as those worn by the Pilgrims are of this type and may be made from a man's pajama pattern or man's jacket pattern (see sections on Vests, Jackets, and Boleros).

For any *period* styles beyond the fifteenth century, and for soldiers' uniforms, it is advisable to include rental for these in planning your budget. There are good costume-rental services in most sizable cities that will ship costumes to distant places. To ensure good rental servcie, the costumer should follow this procedure:

1. Write to the costume-rental company, stating your problem: the kind of costumes wanted, the numbers needed, and the dates of dress rehearsal and performance. Ask for prices and measurement sheets. Do this at least six weeks before your performance if you are sending to some distance.

2. Upon receipt of a reply to your inquiry, fill out measurement sheet accurately, and in your return letter confirm the dates of rehearsal and performance, and confirm the prices quoted.

3. You are then justified in expecting the costumes to arrive before final rehearsal, in good condition, and altered to fit reasonably well. A few adjustments in minor details usually have to be made. The costume-rental company is justified in expecting you to return all costumes and accessories in good condition, well packed, immediately after your production.

Charges for this service vary with localities and concerns and the type of garment demanded.

There are many coats which can be borrowed and many coat problems which attic castoffs can be made to solve. Old frock coats, morning coats, military uniforms, pea jackets, coats for policemen, firemen, milkmen, dentists, and butlers can be borrowed or dug out of trunks. A stitch or two here and there will improve the fit and alter the style somewhat. Old black frock coats and "tails" (if they are given to you) can be sprayed with colored poster paint to change the color and tone.

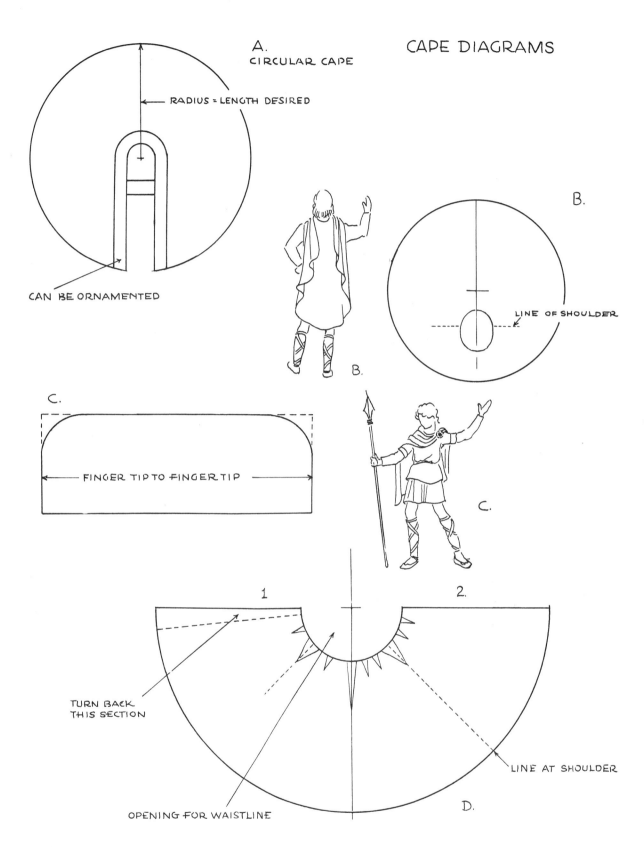

CAPE DIAGRAMS

A.
CIRCULAR CAPE

RADIUS = LENGTH DESIRED

CAN BE ORNAMENTED

B.

B.

LINE OF SHOULDER

C.

FINGER TIP TO FINGER TIP

C.

1   2.

TURN BACK
THIS SECTION

LINE AT SHOULDER

D.

OPENING FOR WAISTLINE

CIRCUM. = 3.14 X DIAM.

DIAGRAM SHOWING HOW
TO ADJUST A SEMICIRCULAR
SKIRT TO USE AS A CAPE.

CAPE DIAGRAMS

SINCE some form of the mantle or cape was the earliest and most persistent form of outer garment in the history of costume, and since there are many needs for it in a wardrobe collection, it is wise for us to know one or two simple methods of construction. It is also wise to have a number of capes, varying in size and color, in any costume collection. No garment, unless it is the tunic, can prove so versatile. From the Dark Ages to the present time it cloaks warriors, kings, men, and women of many social classes. It plays a major rôle in clothing the clergy. It defines the villain as well as Red Riding Hood. It may be as long as the great cape of the musketeer, or as short as a collar; but it almost always is based on the circle or some sector of it. Rectangular drapes were worn as cloaks in the Saxon period or the very early Middle Ages. One is suggested in diagram C. Exact measurements for capes cannot be given, since the length is determined by its use, and the radius of any circular cape is determined by the length desired. Therefore, emphasis is here placed upon the principle of construction rather than on exact measurement.

CIRCULAR CAPE (diagram A)

For the very fullest cape, use a complete circle for a pattern. The radius will be the measurement from the base of the neck to the point where you want the cape to end, plus allowance for finishing. The neck opening for the average close-fitting cape will be based on a circle 18″ in circumference. Since most material will not allow a full circle of any great radius, the full cape will have to be made of two semicircular pieces seamed down center back. The pattern for cutting a semicircular skirt will serve for this cape. It may be ornamented with a band around the neck opening as shown in the illustration of the Bishop's cape (page 50), or around the bottom; or completely around bottom, up the sides of the front, and around the neck. The cape may be single, if of heavy material, but is more durable and richer if lined with a contrasting material.

CIRCULAR CAPE (diagram B)

This cape is an interesting one and a little unusual, as it is designed to be put on over the head, with the sides thrown back over the shoulders to form a kind of cowl neckline. It, therefore, has the head opening off center as shown. If much action is involved, the folds over the shoulder should be tacked to the undergarment, and the center front fastened likewise, or the entire cape will slip out of place. This is beautiful if lined, as the folds create a very graceful pattern down the back. Lining of slightly contrasting tone will heighten this. This cape has further advantages in that it moves beautifully and reveals much of an attractive tunic while it acts as a complement to it.

RECTANGULAR MANTLE (diagram C)

While not so graceful as the circular forms, this kind of covering offers a quick and easy solution to the mantle problem. It is a type used rather commonly in the Dark Ages and Saxon and Norse periods. The rectangle should be as long as the measurement from finger tip to finger tip (arms outstretched) and as wide as from neck to hips, although it may be slightly greater or less in this measurement. Practice draping this as you wish. It is usually fastened on one shoulder with a large brooch, draped loosely over the other, and allowed to fall as it will in the back.

ADJUSTING SEMICIRCULAR SKIRT TO USE AS A CAPE (diagram D)

Since the semicircular cape is cut from the same pattern as the semicircular skirt, with the exception of the neck opening, diagram D shows adjustments to be made if you wish to make a skirt that you may have in your wardrobe serve as a cape. This is a very practical way to secure double duty from a garment.

A woman's normal waistline is about 26-28″. A normal opening for a round neckline is approximately 18″. The left-hand half of diagram 1 suggests that you turn back a small section of the skirt, both for accent and to decrease the circular opening. The rest of the extra material can be taken up in three or four darts: a long, narrow tapered one in center back, a rather wider one at the shoulder line, and very small ones as needed. Or you may follow the right half of the diagram, omitting the turn-back and decreasing the entire semicircle by means of darts. If a loose machine stitch is used, the darts can be released without injury to the garment, and it can again become a skirt.

Note: For openings in a completely circular skirt or cape, a 4½″ radius will give approximately a 28″ circular opening (waistline) and a 2⅞″ radius will give an 18″ opening (neck). For semicircular openings, double these radii. To remove some of the fullness from a circular skirt or cape, dart from the bottom of the cape or skirt to the neck or waistline at construction points such as center front, center back, or at points equidistant from these points on both sides.

Caution: Do not remove the entire amount from one place only, as this will alter the drape of the garment. Rather, take small amounts from the garment at equally spaced intervals.

If you are cutting the cape from new material rather than revamping a skirt, it is advisable to increase the depth of the curve in the back of the garment to about 4″ to ensure an even length. Otherwise, the shoulders will tend to draw the cape up in the center back.

CAPES

16 CENT.

17 CENT.

BISHOP

MONK

CAPES

SIXTEENTH CENTURY

This type of cape is often referred to as the Spanish cape, but was worn in France, Germany, England, and other parts of Europe during this century. In this length, and rather heavily lined and trimmed, it becomes the mark of the nobility. It is extremely full and is cut as a complete or nearly complete circle. It should be of heavy, rich-looking fabric and should be lined. Various collars were used, the most common of which were only slightly curved and stood vertically around the back of the neck. Some capes were fur trimmed. Others had a collar like the one shown, which was cut as part of the front facing and slashed to reveal a colored interlining. These capes often had ornamental bands or embroidery around the bottom, or up the sides of the front, and on the stand-up collar. This trim can be simulated with appliqué of a not too fine sort.

SEVENTEENTH CENTURY

The great cloak of the swashbuckling musketeer is a popular one. It was usually collared for this period, but its descendants which cloak the witch and the villain are most often made without collar. It serves as an example of the long, circular cape of enveloping fullness. While the effectiveness of this cape is increased by cutting it as at least three fourths of a circle, the semicircular pattern, if long, will suffice. Some method of fastening it at the neckline must be considered. Buttons, hooks, or clasps will do ordinarily. For use as a royal garment (for this cape can be medieval as well) the fastening should have ornamental distinction. Brooches, cords, or bands of embroidery may be used. The cape thus caught need not be closed tightly at the neckline, but may be left open in front to disclose the robe beneath. Whatever the fastening in this case, the cape must be secured to the undergarment at the back of the neck, or on the shoulder seams, in order for it to stay in place.

BISHOP'S CAPE

For many Christmas plays and other religious festival processions and pageants there is need for a priestly figure. The great cape of the bishop is a dramatic and beautiful garment. It is cut almost completely circular (see diagram A, page 48) and is richly ornamented with bands of ecclesiastical embroidery as shown. It is rather necessary that some research be done on the robes of the Catholic clergy, as there are liturgical conventions to be observed in the garments worn, the placement of ornament, and even in the colors used in relation to rank and religious season. These established rules, like those of heraldry, are too numerous to be included here. There are many books available on this subject, and in most places there are priests who will be helpful to you in securing the necessary information for a simple suggestion of this type of costume.

MONK

Many religious plays such as *The Juggler of Notre Dame* include monks and nuns. The costume here suggested is drawn from one worn by a Franciscan order, and belongs to this section only by virtue of its round collar, which forms the base of its hood. There are an extraordinary number of variations among the habits of monks and nuns; as many, in fact, as there are established orders. This number of differences is matched only by the provincial variations in peasant costume. For the average play, only the suggestion of belonging to a religious community is necessary. Even the most meticulous realist will find some reduction to general impression necessary. For both monk and nun the basic garment can be a simple, floor length tunic with long, full sleeves. This is held in at the waist with a narrow leather belt (the cincture). In some cases the belting is effected by a cord or rope. Linked to or fastened to the belt on the left side is the rosary. Some kind of rounded collar or cowl, with hood attached, creates a typical neckline. A scapular (a long rectangular panel worn both back and front over the tunic) is often a part of the costume. For the monk, a suggestion of the closely cropped head should be included. The small, round cap is important for this effect. Various veil drapings of a medieval sort distinguish the nuns. Colors vary from white, through the dull greys, grey blues and brown, to black.

THREE TRADITIONAL COSTUMES

13 CENT.

MADONNA

JESTER

THREE TRADITIONAL COSTUMES

THREE costumes often in demand are for the knight, the Madonna, and the jester. Since these do not fall particularly under the divisions of basic costume, they become friendly, if odd, neighbors here.

THE KNIGHT

Since the field of armor and armorial bearings is vast, the amateur costumer quite naturally shies at it. Since accurate representation of the mechanically intricate plate armor of the fifteenth, sixteenth, and early seventeenth centuries is nearly impossible for the amateur to produce, and for the amateur actor to move in easily, illusion is once more the touchstone to successful theatrical effect. The periods in which some form of chain mail was used, namely, the twelfth, thirteenth, and fourteenth centuries, are not difficult to costume. Audiences for the most part are indifferent to the hard and fast lines of knightly heraldry and etiquette, and great liberties may be taken with this costume so long as the ultimate in chivalry is preserved in speech and action. (Indeed, even upon the professional stage there is rarely any real accuracy in this costume.)

The illustration here used is a composite of the outstanding features of the chain-mail periods and does not pretend to identification. The knight of this time wore a hood of mail with a cap helmet of metal; a hauberk, or shirt of mail, often reaching to the knees; several layers of tunics under and on top of the hauberk; hose of chain mail; knee caps; leg shields, sometimes; spurs; belt with sword; and he carried a shield. The chain mail may be simulated by using grey cotton on which small circles of silvered paper are sewn. It is more easily suggested by means of large-mesh dishcloths or mesh curtain material silvered with aluminum paint. This meshed material should be used over grey cotton. Metal pot scrapers of some makes can be unrolled to provide a very usable metal mesh. The cap helmet is made as suggested in the section on Hats and Headdresses, with a circular collar added. Only one tunic is shown here, the top tunic or "surcoat." This should be nearly knee length and may be shorter in front than in the back. This can be of muslin, slip cover fabric, or any similar stuff. Soft, rich color for the tunic, and some painted bands or heraldic device on the breast will add to the decorative effect. Knee caps and leg shields

are best made of leatherette, silvered. While a cape is not usually a part of this costume, it heightens the theatrical effectiveness, especially if there is a large, static group.

MADONNA

The popular conception of this costume has become symbolic. It has come from the representations of the Virgin in the fifteenth century manner of the Italian Renaissance painters, rather than from the original Bethlehem costume. It was simplified by the makers of church images, and traditional color schemes were evolved, until now our customary Madonna wears a simple, floor-length tunic of white or light blue; a nunlike veil (but with the hair showing) of white; a cape or loose cloak, usually of deeper blue, and often lined with rose or pink. We love this figure, and it is meaningful to us, but there is no other reason for considering custom a limitation. Interpretation of the Madonna depends entirely upon the nature of the play. She may be Spanish, Mexican, Medieval English, or simply childlike. She may be early New England, as Lauren Ford has painted her. She may be as dark as the African or Indian conception. She must only be dignified and very lovely.

JESTER

This merry fellow retains his fourteenth century style, which combines a collared hood, a close-fitting jacket, tights, and soft, pointed shoes. The hood is made according to the pattern suggested on description of Insects, page 72, except that a point is allowed for in the cutting. A snow-suit helmet with a round collar may also be used. Any close-fitting woman's-jacket pattern, if extended in length and widened at the bottom, will serve for the jester's coat. The costume seems livelier if the bottom edge is cut in points. One of the fanciful characteristics of the jester is "particolor," the alternation of contrasting color from helmet to shoes. Alternating the color of the whole helmet, jacket, tights, and shoes may substitute for this. Small Christmas bells sewn on the cap and at intervals on the bottom of the jacket are almost a necessity for this prankster. An accessory to the jester is his "bauble" or "zany." This is a little replica of his own head, mounted on a stick and tied with streamers having bells at their ends.

CAPS AND HALOS

13½"

1¼"

7"

4½'   4½"

NURSE'S CAP

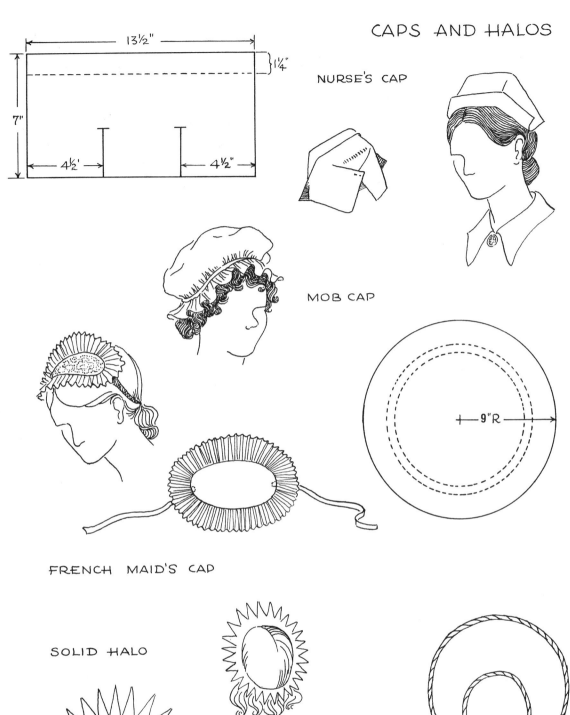

MOB CAP

9"R

FRENCH MAID'S CAP

SOLID HALO

CUT OPENING TO FIT HEAD

WIRE HALO

HATS AND HEADDRESSES

NEVER refuse a hat for which you may have cupboard or box space! Styles may come and go, but hats for the most part are flexible structures and can be reshaped, untrimmed, and retrimmed to adapt themselves to various periods and needs. It is astonishing how often stylists return to Medieval, Renaissance, and Romantic periods for inspiration for the hats of the day. It is surprising how *basic* many of the hat styles are. The little skullcap (calotte); the berets, tams, and Scotch bonnets; the workman's cap, as well as most sports caps and hunting caps with visor and ear flaps, have suffered little change with time and place. Plain, wide-brimmed leghorns and panamas, beavers, and felts have been used for years. The derby, the top hat, the Stetson rancher, and the traditional farmer's straw have kept their identity. Children's bonnets and maids' caps have persisted with surprisingly little variation. All of these, plus the less seemingly adaptable *style* hats, are capable of being punched and bent and twisted into practical illusions of period and national headgear. Even the apparently *impossible* ones offer material such as wire, buckram trims, velvet, feathers, flowers, and ribbons to use in refurbishing the *possible*! So let us sing praises to the patron who calls to say, "I have a number of old hats in my attic. Can you use them?"

PATTERN

Several of the well-known pattern companies offer patterns for the odd little bonnets, caps, hoods, and other soft hats referred to above. Sometimes several designs are included under one number. According to style emphasis, these patterns vary from year to year, and the wise costumer will stock them as they become available.

Since there are a few commonly required headdresses and hats for which patterns are not generally available, the succeeding pages offer some practical diagrammatic drawings of them. These are worked out with measurements for the average size. The reader is asked to consider them as suggestions and to remember always that individual adjustments must be made. The diagrams are designed to provide a few basic forms for hats which can be constructed of paper and lightweight cardboard, such as oak tag. More professional results will be obtained if such hats as the sunbonnet and poke bonnet are cloth-covered. For all the headgear suggested, paper patterns should first be worked out, and adjustments made, before the actual hat is constructed.

CAPS AND HALOS

THE THREE caps shown here are in common use. All of them have many variations, but the methods of construction will be applicable to other similar caps. The nurse's cap and the French maid's cap can be made of paper or cloth, while the mob cap must be made of cloth.

NURSE'S CAP

Measurements for this cap are given in the diagram and need no explanation. Bend back the 1¼" marking to form the front fold, and overlap the two outside 4¼" sections to form the back of the cap. This is usually pinned.

MOB CAP

This cap is used rather generally for maids and nurses of the Victorian era, for many storybook characters such as milkmaids and "grannies," and for little girls of the early nineteenth century. A circular piece of material cut with a 9" radius makes a small cap. About 1½" from the edge place a casing of bias material, and run in elastic. The edge may be pinked or bound with bias tape.

FRENCH MAID'S CAP

While this cap may be of paper for a temporary bit of costume, it is worth while to use cloth, because the cap can be used often in many plays requiring a smart maid. It is simply a small, stiffened oval (about 6" by 2½") covered with fine muslin or dimity, and surrounded with a tightly gathered or pleated frill of cloth or lace. It is tied under the back of the head with dark ribbons.

SOLID HALO

This is often called a "plate halo," as it is a solid piece of lightweight cardboard or buckram with an opening below center to fit the head size. It may be gilded and decorated to suit the fancy. The edge may be broken in any decorative fashion, or a delicate line pattern painted on a plain oval. To secure an accurate opening to fit the head, follow the directions given for the construction of the Puritan hat.

WIRE HALO

This type of halo is much more delicate than the solid one and easier to fit and wear. From many craft-supply houses one can get paper-covered wire which appears to be about ⅛" in diameter, but proves to be very pliable and easy to cut with tin snips. From this or similar wire, form an oval to fit the head size and a large circle. Bind these together at the base. The wire may be gilded or wrapped with strips of metal cloth or ribbon.

CROWNS AND BRIMMED HAT

23"

23"

A.

B.

A.
TOP

2"
8"
10"
23"
LAP
CROWN
B.

C.
BRIM

C.

D.
CROWN

PURITAN OR TAPERED CROWN HAT

CROWNS AND BRIMMED HAT

CROWNS

The simplest type of crown is suggested by diagram A. It is constructed of lightweight cardboard or buckram. This may be covered with metal foil paper or painted with gold or silver paint. Jewels may be folded bits of metal foil, cellophane, fancy buttons, or even gumdrops. This crown is made of a straight strip of paper, approximately 23″ long and as wide as you desire. This measurement will allow for an inch or two of overlap. Fastening may be made by adhesive, thread, or staples.

Crown B shows a variation of the straight crown. The four strips which arch over the head should be an inch wide and 12″ to 13″ long. The accent at the crossing may be a lightweight button or a piece of metal paper.

Crown C should be slightly curved and tapered in order to tie at the base of the neck. Ornamented with paper flowers and streamers, it is a gay sort of crown headdress for spring or peasant dancing figures.

INDIAN HEADDRESS

The feathered headdress of the Indian uses a straight crown not more than 1½″ wide and long enough to fit well down over the forehead. At the center back a tailpiece is constructed of cloth which is about 2″ wide and folded below the point of attachment to hold the feathers in its grip. Feathers, real or of paper, are attached to the crown and tail by sewing or stapling. At the base of each long feather is something to suggest a furry or downy accent. Soft chicken feathers are good. An extra strip of paper cut to simulate these may be substituted. A small tail or reasonable facsimile of such should be placed on either side of the headdress immediately in front of the ear.

PURITAN

This hat has been selected as an example of the tapered, brim hat used not only for Puritans but also for Welsh cos-

tumes, Mother Goose, and similar characters. The way of cutting the brim and securing top to crown and crown to brim is the same for the straight-crown hat, which is simply a strip of material of even measure top and bottom.

The brim, head opening, and top are ovals. To construct these, start with the brim. Using newspaper or brown paper for working out the pattern, describe a circle approximately the size of the outside measurement. Using this as a guide, construct an oval, freehand, by narrowing the sides of the circle and adding to what will become the front and back curves. Then cut the opening for the head by the same method: first a circle, then an oval based on it. To secure a head opening which will fit is the only tricky part of this construction. Start with the head measurement. Let this measure represent the circumference of the inner circle. Recall the formula: Circumference = $3.14 \times d$ (diameter), and you will find that $\dfrac{C \div 3.14}{2}$ will give you a workable radius for the inner circle. For average head measurements this will be 3½″, more or less. On the pattern, trim the oval to secure a good fit.

The crown can be based on a rectangle about 1″ longer than head measurement (about 23″) and wide enough to accommodate the height of crown you desire. The illustration is planned for a crown 8″ high when finished. This requires a width of 10″ for pattern. Mark off two 1″ strips, top and bottom, and construct shallow curves as diagrammed. Slash at 1″ intervals to a 1″ depth both top and bottom. Bend these slashed bits back on the 1″ line in opposite directions, as shown in D, and fasten the lap on the crown. The tabs at the bottom of the crown should then be glued or sewn to the brim. The top of the hat (constructed on the same principle as the head opening, using a smaller measurement), should be glued or sewn to the top of the crown. A cloth band and buckle of silver paper will trim the Puritan hat. A white frill under the brim is a Welsh touch, and who is to say how the Witch is to be accented!

BONNETS

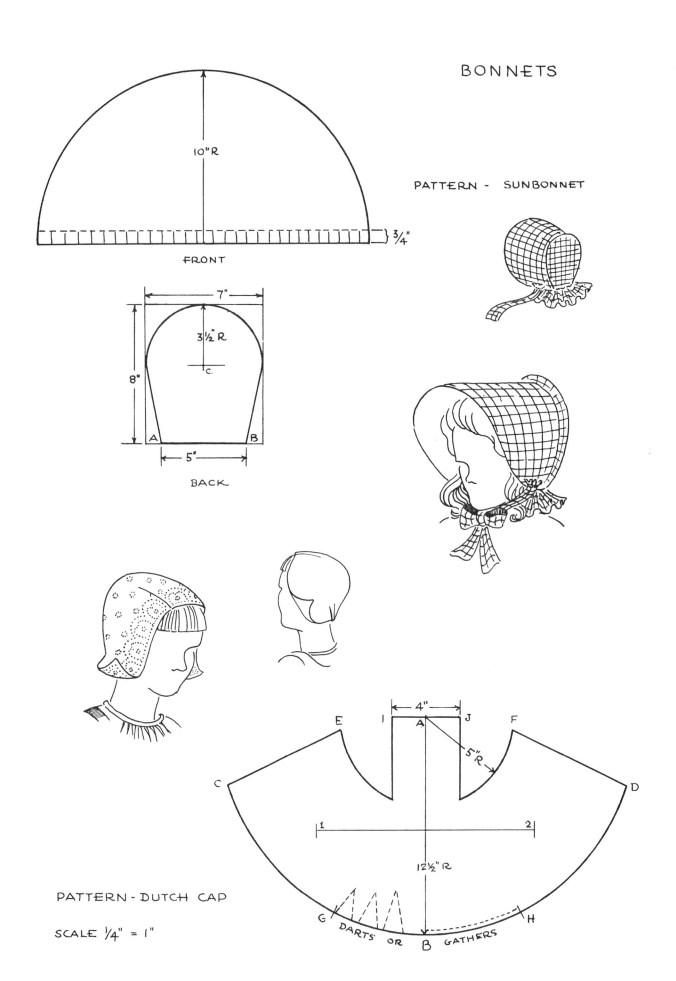

10"R

FRONT

3/4"

PATTERN - SUNBONNET

7"

3½" R

C.

8"

A

B

5"

BACK

PATTERN - DUTCH CAP

SCALE ¼" = 1"

E   I   A   J   F

4"

5"R

C   D

1   2

12½"R

G   DARTS   OR   B   GATHERS

BONNETS

SUNBONNET

A basic pattern for the construction of a simple sunbonnet is here suggested. This one may be made of paper or of some stiff foundation covered with cloth. It may also have a stiff brim and soft back.

A practical, measured pattern for the back is here diagrammed. You may want to vary this somewhat in shape or size or to use a soft cloth back, cut similar in shape to this, but larger and gathered in to fit the straight edge of the brim.

A semicircular shape for the brim is a good one to start with. The base of it (diameter of the circle) is determined by measuring with a tape the distance around the shape of the back from A to B and adding ¾". Slash at 1" intervals to a depth of ¾" along the straight edge. Fold back these tabs. When you curve the brim to fit the back, pin or sew these tabs to the back section. Tie the bonnet on with ribbons or strings of material used for the bonnet. Add a 2" ruffle around the bottom from between points where strings are attached.

As has been suggested before, try out this pattern on newspaper to get exactly what you want. Instead of a true semicircle, you may prefer a shallower curve or a deeper side brim.

DUTCH CAP

This is only one of several possible ways to make a Dutch cap. It should be made of fine muslin, organdy, dimity, or lace and starched before wearing. The pattern should be worked out first with newspaper. Describe the part, C-D, of a circle as shown, using a 12½" radius. From the same center draw another part of a circle, E-F, with 5" radius. Erect a horizontal, I-J, through A and cut off 4" for center front of cap. Drop verticals to touch the 5" circle and cut on these lines. On the large curve the distances C-B and B-D are each 15". From C-E and D-F cut edges a little more than at right angles to outer circle. This will allow E and I, and F and J, to be joined. The distance from G-B and B-H is about 6". Gather or dart G-H until it measures 4". B is center back. Join the smaller curves at E and F to the 4" center front piece. C and D then become the tips of the wings and should be curled back when finished. The distance from 1-2 is taken from ear tip to ear tip and is merely a guide to relative size. Since this cap does not fit tightly, these measurements may be varied somewhat.

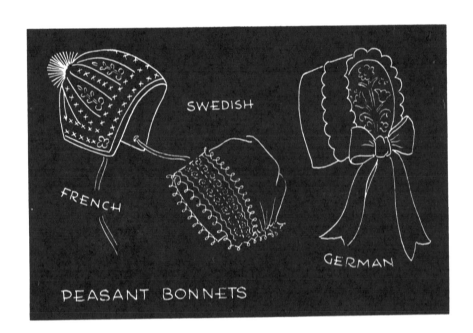

PEASANT BONNETS

SWEDISH

FRENCH

GERMAN

HATS BASED ON THE CIRCLE

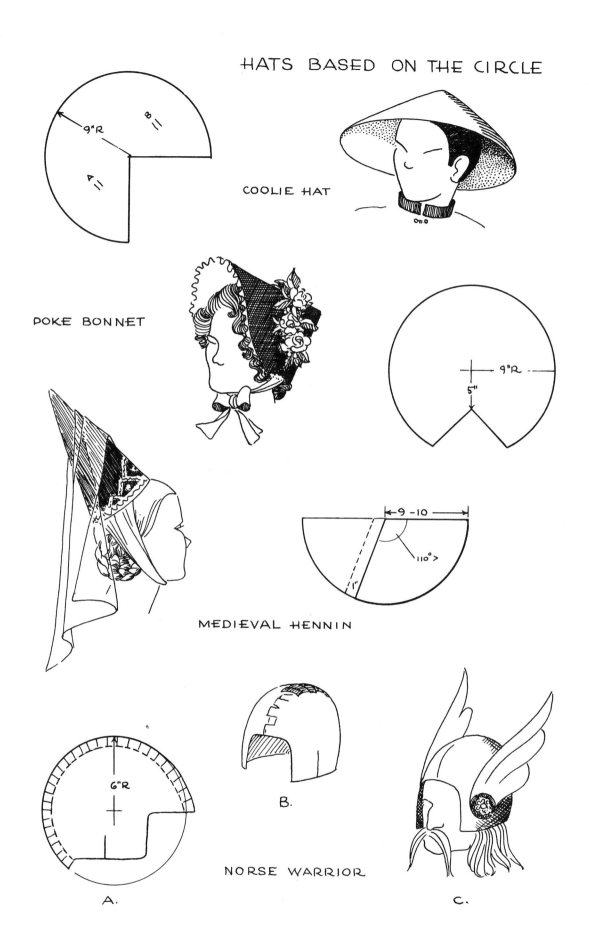

COOLIE HAT

POKE BONNET

MEDIEVAL HENNIN

NORSE WARRIOR

A.

B.

C.

HATS BASED ON THE CIRCLE

ALL FOUR of the hats here illustrated are made from circles or parts of them. They may all be constructed of paper, but the poke bonnet is of more permanent value than the others; accordingly, as a hat to use for more than one performance, it deserves to be cloth covered. Lightweight cardboard or several thicknesses of newspaper machine-stitched together are suitable materials.

COOLIE HAT

Three quarters of a circle with a 9″ radius makes this hat. Overlap and fasten the two cut edges, attach tapes through slits at A and B. Tie the hat on either under the chin or at the back of the neck. It may be painted a straw color and sprayed or painted to suggest texture.

POKE BONNET

The very simplest suggestion for this type of hat is here given. From the center of a circle with 9″ radius, measure down 5″ and make a right-angled, pie-shaped cut as shown. Overlap the cut edges to form the short back of the bonnet, and tie on with ribbons. A ruffle under the brim softens the face line. Flowers may be tacked to the outside to suggest a crown, or placed inside the brim to frame the face.

If a cloth-covered hat is desired, cut two pieces of material exactly the shape of the pattern but ¾″ larger. Stitch together, wrong sides out, and turn. Insert stiffened base and proceed as above. Old straw hats with even brims may quite easily be transformed into poke bonnets by trimming off the brim in the back to about 1″ at base of neck, and binding the edge. It is then worn well back on the head, tied under the chin, and trimmed as you will.

MEDIEVAL HENNIN

This form of headdress has become a stereotyped conception of what was worn by the court ladies of medieval days. As a matter of fact, it was only one of many forms of head covering, and worn only in the latter part of the period. Since it is utterly fantastic, popular acceptance gives it the power to identify an atmosphere as medieval. Most headdresses of this period almost completely covered the hair. Often a jeweled snood hid the hair; quite often some form of cap or draped veil was worn under the hennin or similar headdress. This illustration is presented without these additions to show more clearly the construction of the hennin itself. It is of the "steeple hat" or dunce-cap style and is made of a cone. A good cone is constructed by cutting off about 110 degrees of a semicircle described with a 9 or 10″ radius, plus an inch added as shown for overlap. Hennins were often much larger than this, but the long ones, especially if draped, became very awkward to wear. This cone-shaped hat is best kept on with a wide, crushable cloth band fastened under the chin. If hat is made of cardboard, it can be painted any color to match or contrast with the costume. Pattern may be painted on or worked out with cotton yarn glued to the hat. Very transparent veiling or China silk should be draped over the point. Often drapery fluttered from the very tip of the hennin. As was suggested before, a soft veil over the head and under the hat is appropriate and necessary to give real period effect.

NORSE OR SAXON HELMET

Head covering for warriors of the Dark Ages, as well as some for the Roman and medieval armed figures, were of the helmet type. This one was selected as being possible to diagram clearly. It may be said in passing that a head covering of this helmet type is easier to make of cloth, or can even be simulated by using a heavy rubber bathing cap treated to a coat of aluminum paint. To these helmets, wings and crests may be added. For children's plays, helmets may be made of stout paper or tag board or buckram, according to the accompanying diagram. Cut two pieces as in diagram A. The 6″ radius gives a good average size. Slash at 1″ intervals to a depth of about ¾″ to allow for overlapping and fitting the curve in joining the two pieces. Starting at the forehead interlace the tabs as shown. Pin these and later glue or stitch them. As you approach the top of the helmet, overlap the tabs a trifle to round the helmet from neck to crown, and pin securely. You may want to slash the helmet just behind the ear and overlap the side pieces to help curve the helmet in toward the bottom. After the entire joining has been effected, glue or sew the joint and reinforce it with gummed tape.

Once more—the recommendation is to work this out in newspaper first to get the tricks of joining!

For the Norse or Saxon warrior, wings of cardboard or buckram can be attached at the sides. A crest for the Roman soldier may be constructed on the principle of the rooster comb (see plate for Birds, page 70). A resourceful person can devise variations on the shape of this helmet to suit period needs. For more complicated armored headgear it will be necessary to consult more highly specialized books such as those listed in the Bibliography.

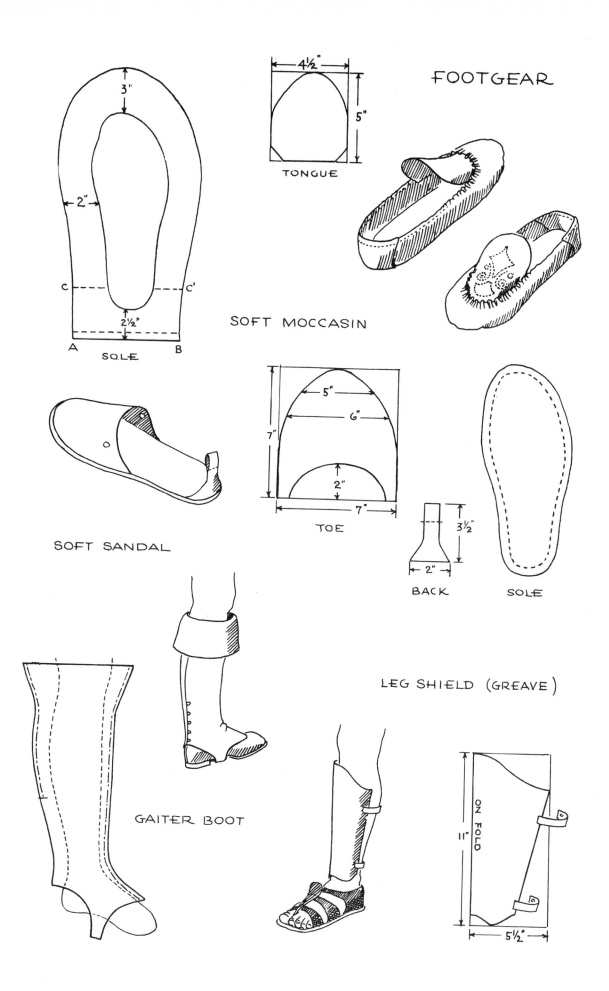

FOOTGEAR

3"

2"

C — C'

2½"

A   SOLE   B

4½"

5"

TONGUE

SOFT MOCCASIN

SOFT SANDAL

5"

6"

7"

2"

7"

TOE

3½"

2"

BACK   SOLE

GAITER BOOT

LEG SHIELD (GREAVE)

ON FOLD

11"

5½"

FOOTGEAR

So MUCH can be said and, indeed, has been written about the footgear of all times and places that it is a tremendously difficult task to make a few brief recommendations.

For all plays, whatever their nature, and for any indoor production, however spectacular, it is rather important that the actors tread silently. So few amateur stages are equipped with floor cloths, that the costumer is wise who solves her foot problems with soft shoes. Feet of many periods can be satisfactorily shod with ballet slippers, leather dance sandals, soft play shoes, bedroom slippers, moccasins, children's sandals, and even with stockings alone; so it is a great help to the costumer to have a generous supply of these in the wardrobe collection. Many actors prefer to furnish their own shoes, and in amateur productions they are often required to do so. Under some circumstances this is a troublesome business; and since the soft shoes mentioned can be sent to cleaners, a collection of them is practical. These may be changed occasionally by dyeing, painting, or gilding them. Other shoes, oxfords, pumps, and low-heeled party shoes not practical to keep in storage, can be transformed by the addition of buckles and laces. Many pairs of cotton stockings are another great asset in the costume wardrobe. These must be washed after each performance and may be dyed again and again as long as they wear.

Sandals, rhythm sandals, and all sorts of cloth play shoes of the sandal type may serve to suggest Egyptian overseers and nobility, Greek and Roman athletes and warriors, Biblical shepherds, peasants, Renaissance and Elizabethan nobles.

Ballet slippers, either laced or plain, are appropriate for early nineteenth century ladies and children, for most storybook characters, the ladies of the Crinoline Period, and circus performers. Simple, heelless bedroom slippers can be used for the same purposes if tongues are cut off and trimming removed.

Soft cloth shoes, such as felt and quilted slippers ("scuffy type"), or felt and flannel moccasins without soles can quite easily be made. These with felt boots, made over a stocking shape, or "boot socks," are fine for warriors of the Dark Ages and peasants of many periods. Pointed felt boots can easily be made over a stocking pattern for characters of the Middle Ages. An easier solution for this period is simply an extra pair of stockings to be worn as a soft shoe. These should be slightly long in the foot, and then the toe can be pointed and a piece of buckram inserted as a sole which will fit into the point and stiffen it a little. Stockings worn this way should be rolled to the ankle. To form higher boots they should be cut off where desired, and held with elastic. Dark stockings may be used for many boot purposes and can even be cut to suggest straps across the shin bone, if the cut edges are immediately "stopped" with lacquer or shellac.

Leggings, gaiters, spats, and boots are in common demand. You can borrow or beg spats and boots, or you can use the currently popular rubber "rain boot" to very good advantage.

Leg shields, puttees, and strappings are easily taken care of. Leg shields (greaves), which were a part of the equipment of many warriors, are easy to make, and are illustrated in the accompanying drawings. Soldiers' puttees are constructed on the same principle. Strapping for cross-gartering the average shepherd or medieval peasant will have to be at least three yards long for each leg. Start with the center of the strap under the instep, cross the bands several times front and back until the knee is reached, and wrap straight at least twice to hold the gartering in place. Since bias strips stay in place better than straight ones, a very practical thing to do with flannel and muslin scraps left from costume-making is to convert them into folded bias strips 1½" wide and put them away for future use.

SOFT MOCCASIN

While this particular diagram is planned as a soft shoe for Indian costume, it is equally practicable for other uses. A flatter tongue, without decoration, will make it suitable for Norse warriors and medieval peasants. This moccasin should be made of soft but strong material. Flannelette (used double), khaki, denim, or cotton slip cover fabric are all suitable.

Start by drawing around the foot for a pattern. Lay this on the material and mark off an enlarged shape as shown. Extend this about 3" at the toe end, 2½" at heel, and 2" the rest of the distance. Turn a ⅛" hem (single) across the straight heel. With the foot in place, turn up the heel section and make mitred corners at C and C¹. Pin and sew these down firmly. This will mean lifting up the sides at these points to join the heel. Starting at C¹, turn under the edge once and gather around to C. Draw this up to fit the foot, and fasten securely. Adjust the fullness so that as much of it as possible comes over the toe end. Cut tongue and insert under the fullness in front, and stitch in place. The tongue may be double or lined with crinoline if you want to feature it in the Indian costume. Painted decoration to suggest beadwork may be added.

SOFT SANDAL

A very simple sandal to use for many costumes is based on the "scuffy" bedroom slipper, and has a small tab at the heel through which a tape may be passed to hold the slipper firmly on the foot. These are similar to "rhythm sandals" and may be made of leather, leatherette, oilcloth, denim, or quilted fabric. Two layers of denim, with quilt-wadding between them, and machine-stitched to "quilt" them together, make a firm and more comfortable shoe, worth the extra trouble.

The sole is cut about ½″ larger all around than the shape of the foot. The toe and heel pieces are cut as diagrammed, and sewn to the sole on the outside line. These seams must be strong. Overcasting with button thread, or binding, will make them firm. All edges must be overcast or treated with shellac to prevent fraying. Bend back 1″ of heel tab and stitch to form loop. Eyelets may be added to toe section, as shown, and tape laced through these, crossing over the arch of the foot and passing through the heel loop.

GAITER BOOT

This kind of gaiter worn over inconspicuous shoes is a great help in creating colonial soldiers, cavaliers, Puss in Boots, giants, and many storybook characters. Without the cuff, and carefully fitted, it is suitable for many early nineteenth century characters, particularly the clergy. For this foot accessory, heavy, firm material is best. Vinyl is good, especially if a shiny effect is wanted. Leatherette and similar compositions give a splendid effect but are difficult to handle unless you have a strong machine needle. Interlining of a dark color may be used, or flannelette, if doubled.

First cut a pattern of paper (2 pieces), shaping it in relation to a stocking of the proper size. Leave generous allowance for seam and solidity of the leg, especially at mid-calf. Try this pattern on the leg of the wearer before making it in cloth, as individual measurements vary. For the average adult you will need at least 6″ in pattern width at the ankle and 9″ at mid-calf. A rough fitting will prove where you need to increase or decrease these measurements. Stitch the two pieces of cloth together as shown by the dot-dash line, leaving the boot-back open just below mid-calf. Fit and fasten the tab under the instep, and close the boot down the open part of the back with a zipper or hooks and eyes. If you prefer, the boot or gaiter may be opened all the way up the outside with a zipper; but long zippers add to the cost and are difficult to turn over if you want a turned-back cuff. Unless the boot is very tight-fitting at the knee, you will need to hold it in place with an elastic band. The cuff may be lined with a contrasting color if that fits into your schemes.

LEG SHIELDS (GREAVES)

Some variation of this structure is a part of many warrior costumes. They can be made of buckram, lightweight cardboard, leatherette, or some similar material. A suggested average-size pattern with measurements is given. Cut this to fit the individual measurement, trimming it to leave ankle bone free for movement. Bands of elastic will hold the shield in place, or bands of material fastened with snaps may be used. The shields may be painted with aluminum paint to become part of an armored costume.

FANTASTIC COSTUMES

IT IS when we face the birds and the bees, the rooster, the elephant, the tiger, that our knees begin to quiver. But the necessity of considering the flower, the fruit, and even the vegetable gives one a veritable ague. We feel vaguely at home with elves and fairies. We have faint images of witches, ghosts, devils, and angels in our memories. But except for hazy recollections of Greek-like draperies, we draw a blank page from that memory book when called upon for allegories and abstractions: Truth, Justice, Fire, and Famine. For these there is no established prototype except for the use of symbolic color. Imagination, good taste, and simplicity should act as controls for these interpretations.

There is little source material in costume books to which one may cling in these emergencies. From one point of view this is an advantage, because it frees us all from a conventional or standardized representation of those characters, which are by nature fanciful and are best and freshest when drawn from individual imagination. The following pages of more or less diagrammatic nature would seem to belie the preceding statement, but the drawings and explanations are offered in the spirit of practical suggestion and do not, even in measurement, try to establish a commandment.

Two facts in the solution of all imaginative costume problems which are necessary to consider are these: First, that all theatre is *illusion*, not reality, and second, that good illusion depends upon good *design*. Creating the illusion of an animal character is more important than any attempt at accurate representation, which is impossible anyway where animals, flowers, and vegetables are concerned, because of physical limitations. This forces us to approach any of these characters from the design standpoint, asking and seeking solution to the following questions:

1. What are the outstanding characteristics of the animal, flower, bird, etc.?

    Nature—noisy, rowdy, tame, comical

    Texture—rough, smooth

    Action—hopping, running, waddling

    Color—bright, dull, identifying coloration

2. What is the unique feature to emphasize?
   A long bill
   A mane
   Pointed ears
   Trunk
   Bulging eyes
3. How can I adjust these identifying characteristics to the human figure?
4. How can I best create the *illusion* of this character without also creating discomfort or embarrassment for the actor?
5. With what available materials can I suggest the color and texture of my character?

The imagination of the very small child is so vivid as to almost preclude the necessity of costume for simple dramatization. However, he dearly loves a paper mask, a shawl thrown over the shoulders, or some other simple changing of the *status quo*, more for novelty than of necessity. The older child and the adult are most often self-conscious in the interpretation of fanciful characters. Nothing is as effective in changing self-consciousness to ease, and even abandon, as a completely enveloping costume, a hood, a mask. If you doubt this, uncover some adult prankster next Halloween.

The following pages offer typical solutions to a few of these "sticklers." Let us hope that they will be only a springboard to other ways of meeting the demands for animation. If you can make a mask or a hood or a tail, who is to dictate the humor or the whimsy its shape or length will accommodate? If you can devise a new wing for an angel, who is to say you are exaggerating? Who is so dead as not to enjoy a new ghost?

FOUNDATIONS FOR ANIMAL COSTUMES

SINCE most animal characters are used to heighten the satirical or whimsical aspects of a play, or for pure delight in a make-believe situation, their appearance can and ought to deviate from the normal. Exaggeration, even distortion, of their distinctive features should be sought and employed except where it might interfere with free body movement or clarity of speech.

A satisfactory basic garment for many animal costumes seems to be one similar to a one piece child's sleeping garment or snow suit, with feet and hands covered. Some pattern companies carry a pattern of this type. The pattern may or may not include a hood. The animal costume should have a close fitting head covering to serve as a foundation to which ears, manes and other accessories can be attached. The helmet is most secure if it is firmly attached to the neck band. For this reason, it is simpler if the garment opens down the front. Where a hood is unnecessary, as is the case with a false head, the garment may be opened down the back. Openings must be securely fastened. Zippers or Velcro, a nylon fabric fastener are ideal fasteners. Crotches should be reinforced by double stitching or otherwise strengthened by seam binding.

Animal characters are often comfortably dressed in leotards or tights with accessories such as hoods with ears, tails, wings, ruffs, and even one or two items of human clothing such as a vest, a tail coat or an apron to suggest the character. For instance, the Red Riding Hood wolf villain might have a cape and top hat!

For many animals, particularly if they have long speaking assignments, the face may be left uncovered and a stylized make-up used. Some are better suggested by the use of a face mask, or even a half-mask which leaves the mouth free. Very grotesque effects may demand an entire false head. This is a more difficult type of disguise to make and to wear and should be used only if there is very little speaking to be done by the wearer. A false head should be constructed with great attention to placement of mouth and eye openings. Suggestions for the construction of such a head are given in the section on Masks, page 83.

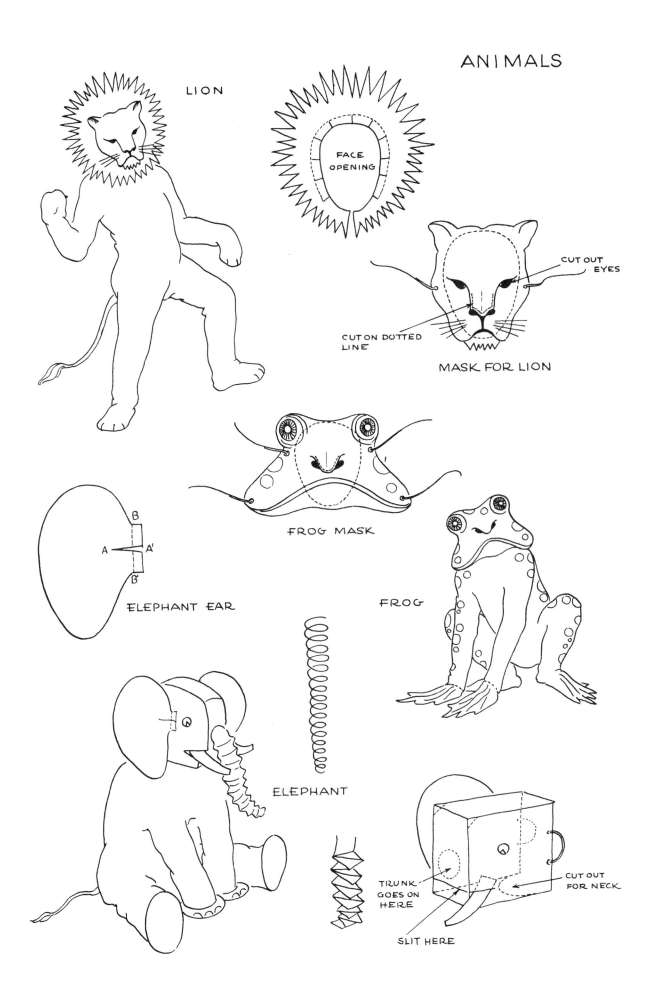

LION

FACE OPENING

CUT OUT EYES

CUT ON DOTTED LINE

MASK FOR LION

FROG MASK

ELEPHANT EAR

FROG

ELEPHANT

TRUNK GOES ON HERE

CUT OUT FOR NECK

SLIT HERE

ANIMALS

LION

The foundation as described above may be of brown flannel. For this costume a hood is needed. A simple face mask of construction paper or buckram gives complete disguise. The diagram of a suggested mask shows by the dotted oval the size relationship of mask to face. The dotted line around the nose indicates a cut to be made. If the flap thus released is slightly folded on the center line and across the beginning of the cut, it will accommodate the pushing out of the nose. The mask is more interesting if it is lighter than body color. There are numerous ways to suggest a mane or ruff. Frayed rope may be attached to the hood. A mass of curled paper may likewise be sewn to the headpiece. A very simple flat paper ruff is here suggested with a diagram of its cut. Around the face opening make several slits about 1" deep, and bend back paper on the dotted line. This gives you something to attach to the hood. You may have to reinforce this area with cloth or paper tape. Tailors' mending tape may be applied with a hot iron. The ruff is decoratively interesting if it is different in color or tone from mask and body. It might even be of dull orange and the color repeated in the plume of the tail.

FROG

A flannelette, hooded foundation, dyed green, is the suggested basis here. It is effective if there is a variation in the green, so do not work hard to dye evenly. A simple face mask is suggested. This can be tied firmly around the head by the upper strings and loosely fastened with the lower strings to bend the mask only slightly toward the back. Holes for the eyes cannot correspond to the frog's eyes, so they must be planned in relation to the face. Perhaps the nostrils can be cut out to serve, or additional openings made. These may be disguised as spots or frankly left as functional cuts. The nose is cut as described in the lion mask. Separate glove-like hand and foot coverings may be fastened to the sleeves and bottoms of legs or worn as gloves. These should be large and web-like in structure. Spots may be painted on back and toward the front of the garment, leaving the belly lighter.

ELEPHANT

For this bulky animal the foundation should be quite loose and baggy and not necessarily hooded. The actor may be padded, but freedom of action must be considered. Since the large clumsy head of this beast is one of the distinctive features, an entire head covering is suggested. For a very finished production, heads could be made as described in the section on Masks, page 83. But for simple performances a very satisfactory covering can be effected by means of a paper-bag head. Ordinary shopping bags are strong and a good size for the child actor. The sketch on the accompanying diagram sheet needs explanation. The bottom of the bag becomes the front of the face. Cut a slit in this well below the middle and bend down the part becoming the lower jaw. Tusks of cardboard or rolled paper may be fastened inside upper jaw. The upper corners of the bag should be crushed or folded over to suggest a rounded forehead. A neck opening is cut (shown by dotted line) in the bottom side, at open end of the bag, to allow the head to get nearer the front of bag. The handles may be used to fasten the back (top) of the bag together. Large ears are cut of tag board, with flaps bent back for fastening them on the sides of the bag. These ears should be partially split (cut A-A¹) and the sections overlapped to create a slight three-dimensional effect. The trunk offers some difficulty in solution. Two suggestions are here offered. A piece of soft wire may be coiled and inserted in a grey cotton stocking and fastened to the front of the face. A large "cat-stair" of folded paper may be fastened to the "face." The "cat stair" is made by joining long strips of construction or brown wrapping paper at right angles, the pieces overlapping. These pieces should be approximately four inches wide by six feet long. These pieces are then folded over one another alternately at right angles until the length has been used up and the ends fastened with staples or paste. The strips, if carefully cut, may be tapered to make a smaller end for the trunk. Directions for making a "cat stair" are given in many paper construction books. Either the coil of wire or the "cat stair" will provide a flexible trunk.

The entire head is then painted to match the costume. A wispy tail is needed, and legs, longer than usual in sleeping garments, may be attached to cardboard ovals an inch longer than the actor's feet. These are not necessary but are amusing. To see out of this head is difficult, so experiment is necessary to get practical eye openings. The entire costume is clumsy, but so is an elephant!

EARS AND THREE MASKS

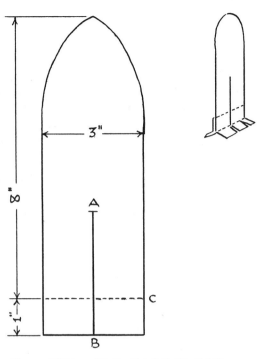

3"

8"

A

C

B

1"

PATTERN FOR RABBIT EAR

I

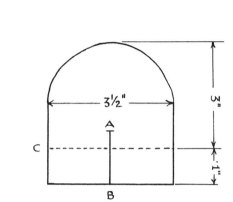

3½"

3"

A

C

B

1"

EAR PATTERN TO USE
FOR MANY ANIMALS

II.

III PATTERN FOR CAT EAR

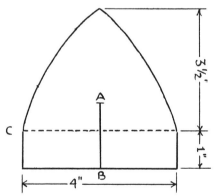

3½"

A

C

B

1"

4"

EARS AND THREE MASKS

THE ACCOMPANYING diagram offers patterns useful in constructing ears for various animal hoods. As has been said before, the faces particularly of child actors may be left uncovered, and indeed this is advisable for many costumes in the fanciful category. It is therefore rather necessary that all other additions to the costume tell the story. Ears are a distinctive feature and should be carefully considered and constructed.

RABBIT

The measurements are only suggestive of a practical size and may well be altered for varying sizes and effects. The rabbit ear may be made of cloth matching the costume, in which case it should be made double and reinforced with crinoline or a fine wire sewn along the outside edge to make it stand up. These reinforcements must be fastened securely to the helmet to ensure a vertical position for the ears. The inside of the ear may be pink for a white rabbit or buff for a brown one. If cloth is used, 8″ is long enough, as the bottom can be pleated to make the ear concave. This pleating can be sewn to the hood.

The ears may be made of construction paper and painted. If paper is used, it will be necessary to split the ear on line A-B and overlap the bottom sections to form the concavity. For paper, fold back on dotted line C to form a base which can be fastened to the hood. Another piece of paper should be fastened to the back of the bottom and bent opposite to the front. This will give a more secure base for the long ear. Similar reinforcements may be used for other shorter ears but are rarely necessary, as the short ears hold their shape easily and do not cause the strain on the hood which comes with the long ears.

GENERAL TYPE OF EAR (For such animals as the lion, bear, lamb, etc.)

These are usually squarish, with a more rounded tip. The construction is exactly like that of the rabbit ear.

PATTERN OF EAR FOR CAT

The construction and material suggested is the same as above. Cats' ears should be slightly longer and much more triangular than others. The overlapping at the bottom should be greater to give greater depth to the structure.

At the bottom of the page are sketches to remind the costumer that dogs vary in essential head shape more than most other animals. Here we have the long, triangular dog head, the round dog head, and the rectangular dog head. These sketches may be used as suggestions for varied types of dog masks.

ADDITIONAL MASKS

TYPICAL BIRD
COSTUME

BIRDS

BACK

PATTERN FOR BEAK

6"

9"

WINGS

3"

CUT TO FIT NECK OPENING

ROUGHLY THE DISTANCE FROM
FINGER TIP TO FINGER TIP

PATTERN FOR COMB

FOLD OF PAPER
REINFORCED

A.

B.

COSTUME FOR ROOSTER

BIRDS

THE VERY IDEA of a human body representing a bird form is a fantastic one. Therefore it behooves us to capitalize on the imagination which an audience is always ready to project into a play, the characters of which must, necessarily, depart from strict reality. We should consider, primarily, those features which will create illusion of character rather than to struggle against nature.

For all general purposes the same foundation garment as suggested for animals may be used for birds. Leg wrappings may be added if the costumer chooses this concession to a naturally slim leg. Or tights and tunic may be substituted for the sleeping garment. The important features of the costume for the child actor are the wings. Wings alone are often enough to make the young actor feel birdlike. For a finished production a little further illusion of character is desirable, so let us consider the problems of wings, head covering with bill, and one or two other "accessories" such as combs, wattles, eyes, and tails.

TYPICAL BIRD COSTUME (General Use)

Using the suggested foundation garment in appropriate color for the kind of bird called for, add the same kind of hood or helmet used for animal costumes. It is most practical to have this tight-fitting around the face, add a bill like a visor to the forehead section, and forget a face mask. The bill may be made of heavy construction paper or tag board and painted, since it always contrasts with the texture and color of the head. A pattern for the bill is here diagrammed. Measurements are only suggested. Slash at 1″ intervals to a 1″ depth at bottom of the bill. Be sure one of these slashes is on the center line, as the bill should be creased on that line for accent. Bend back the slashed bits on the dotted line and let them overlap to form a curve. These tabs may then be inserted under the forehead section of the hood and sewn firmly to it.

There are many ways of constructing wings. Two solutions are here shown: one, for a full pair of wings, attached by a neckpiece (collar) sewn to the back of the neck opening and fastened in front; the other, as shown below with rooster costume, is merely a single wing attached to the sleeve of the garment. This is cut to more or less fit the shoulder seam of the garment and should be sewn to the sleeve on line A-B. Either type of wing may be made of cloth match-ing the garment, stiffened with crinoline or several thicknesses of paper stitched between the layers of material. Wire sewn around the edge of the wings may be used either with or without the other stiffening. The long, paired wings are attached by tapes sewn to the wing tips to tie around the child's wrists. The wings may be attached to center back line if added support is necessary.

If a tail is desired, one can be constructed by the same principle as suggested for the bill, and attached to the waistband in the back. Suggestion of feathers may be secured by painting or by sewing leaflike shapes of cloth or paper on the body or wings. This is an added complication, and use of it depends upon whether your interest is in silhouette or texture. Eyes may be painted or appliquéd on the hood.

ROOSTER

Poultry problems need a few added considerations. There are variations of bills and combs and wattles and distin-guishing tails such as we find in the rooster, peacock, and turkey. Here resourcefulness and imagination are more important than recipe. The methods used to construct the suggestion of Rooster are applicable to other forms. The comb is made according to the principle of the bill, and like the bill can be made of cloth or paper. If paper is used, be sure that it is double, and of a shape similar to the pattern illustrated. Slash the bottom (part which will fasten to the hood) as the bill was slashed. Bend each side back on the dotted line and overlap slashed section to fit the curved surface. The tabs are sewn down to the helmet or hood. A dash of red paper or cloth, like a floppy bow tie, will suggest the wattle. An amusing tail for the rooster may be made by using several sheets of folded paper. Brown wrapping paper or newspaper is suitable. Using the fold as a starting point, draw a tail similar to the one here suggested. Open the fold, and with a large machine stitch, sew the folds of paper to an inch strip of strong material. This strip is fastened down the lower back of the garment, as shown. The feathers can then be roughly painted and allowed to fall free. Make the tail smaller rather than larger than in its natural relationship to the body, in order to avoid too much reinforcement of the feathers. They get "floppy" if too large. Paint will give them extra body.

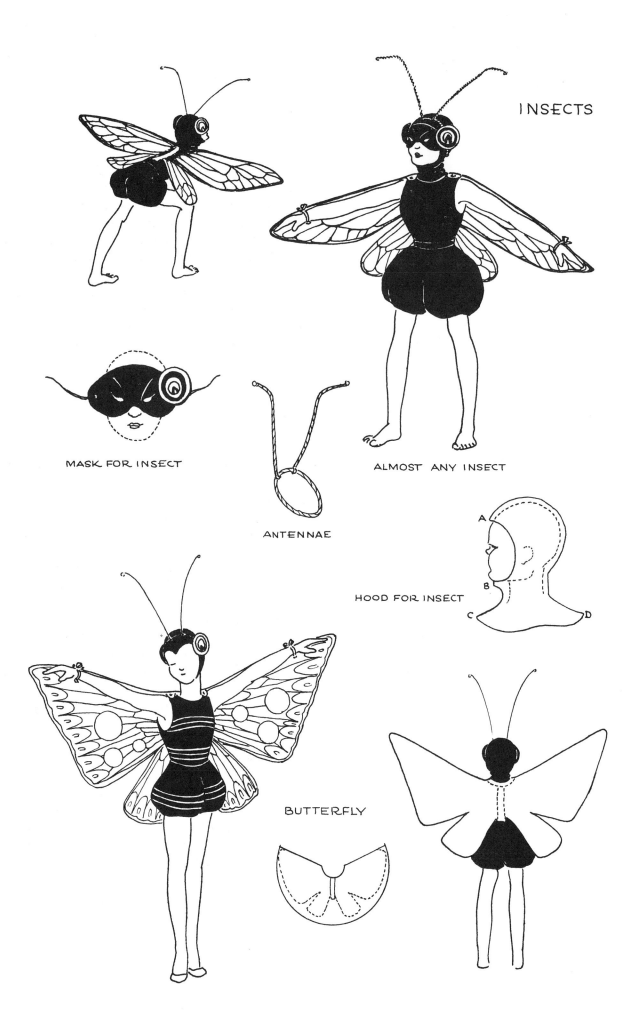

INSECTS

MASK FOR INSECT

ANTENNAE

ALMOST ANY INSECT

HOOD FOR INSECT

BUTTERFLY

INSECTS

THE BUTTERFLIES and ants and bees present slightly different problems from those of the animals and birds. Many times for the sake of economy the sleeping-garment foundation is used for a body covering. This, however, seems a trifle clumsy, since by their very nature insects have delicate appendages. The suggestion here offered is to use a cotton jersey sports shirt and bloomers of matching color. There is no real reason why arms and legs should be covered unless a mass effect of dark is desired. Children's thin arms and legs are often delightfully awkward, and this may be capitalized. One of the outstanding characteristics of all insects is the bulbous, segmented body. Slight padding of the chest area and some stuffing in the bloomers will help to create this effect, especially if the waistline is constricted by a tight belt. Heads should be covered by head or cap to disguise the hair and provide a base for the antennae. Half-masks can increase the grotesque appearance of the creature. Prominent eyes, high and to the side of the head, are necessary even if they become an additional pair to the human ones masked or uncovered. Audiences will accept this multiplicity with delight. The large insect eyes may be made of paper fastened on the hood or mask so that they are slightly curved. Sometimes segments of large, soft rubber balls may be sewn on the hood.

Wing patterns can be made from a semicircular piece of material, reinforced down the center fold for fastening to the garment down the center of the back to stand the strain of the wings. Near the tips of the wings fasten tapes to tie around the wrists. The wings of insects should be delicate, and offer an opportunity to try out some of the new transparent and semitransparent plastic materials. Edges of these should be bound to prevent tearing. A soft wire (flower wire) may be sewn in with the binding to stiffen the edges. For a soft wing, reinforce only the edges which attach to the body and let the rest fall free.

Biology books with good illustrations are most helpful to a designer of insects and a painter of wings. A record of what nature has provided is a marvelous springboard for the imagination.

ALMOST ANY INSECT

Using the romper foundation, or tights with a helmet as head covering and a stiffened wing, this plan needs only the addition of a half-mask or weird face make-up and antennae. The half-mask should be planned to fit the face, as shown in the diagram. Eye slits should be unusual in shape. Slanting them upward is a good idea. They should not be emphasized, as the round false eyes must make the dominant impression. Circles of paper painted with concentric rings and center can be fastened on the side flaps of the mask. Fastened so that the circle bulges slightly, it will help to create the exaggeration

from the front view. A very simple way to make the antennae and hold them in place is to make an oval of paper-covered wire which fits snugly around the head like the band of a hat. To this, about 4″ apart at center front, twist two delicate wires to stand up and turn slightly outward. These may be wrapped in metallic cloth or painted gold, silver, or color. Slight accents at the tips are effective. Be careful to wrap the junction of antennae and head band or the "bumps" will press uncomfortably on the forehead.

BUTTERFLY

As one of the most loved of the insects, the butterfly offers opportunity for a rather free play of the imagination in shape and color. The body may be made very decorative with painted stripes, but should be simple in order to throw emphasis on the wings. Only one type of wing is here illustrated. Consult any one of the many books on butterflies and you will find countless variations to choose from. Children take great joy in these illustrations, and often are able to provide real specimens from a collection to use as source material. A delicate fabric ought to be used for the wings, and the cut suggested is one based on an area slightly greater than a half circle. This allows enough fullness for free, large movements of the arms. The length of the line A-B is a little more than the distance from neck to finger tip. The inner curve of the circle should fit the back of the neck line. Decoration may be painted on the wings and may be imaginative but conforming to, rather than opposing, the natural construction of the butterfly wing.

The face is best left uncovered and a "pretty" make-up rather than a weird one should be used. The hair should be covered. An old bathing cap with an exaggerated center point is ideal for this. Antennae are made as described above, and ought to further the effect of delicacy.

HELMET

The making of a helmet for head covering may here be described. Draw a silhouette of the child's head by casting a shadow on a piece of white paper. Draw a curved line A-B from the forehead around the temples to jaw line and well forward under the chin. Describe a curve to form shoulder piece which will be tucked into the neck of the bloomer. Allow about an inch all around this outline and cut two paper patterns. Pin these carefully and adjust to the head of the actor. Then cut the cloth pieces and stitch together from A-D. Leave the edges B-C open. The helmet may be hooked under the chin. If you prefer using a commercial pattern, there are several types made available by commercial-pattern companies. These are usually found as part of a child's snow suit pattern.

FLOWERS

DAISY

SWEET PEA

VIOLET

LILY

NASTURTIUM

10°

CUT TO FIT NECK
OPENING

CLOVER COLLAR

CLOVER

FLOWER COSTUME

FLOWERS

MANY PLAYS and festival celebrations for children include flower characters, and these always pose a peculiar problem to the costumer. The problem involves the question of whether to *represent* the flower or to *suggest* it. Since it is an impossible feat to really reproduce a likeness to any flower, because of body construction and need for action, any attempt at realism is defeated at its beginning. But let us take heart, for there are many ways of suggesting the characteristics and the spirit of various flowers in complete harmony with the functional demands of costume. To approach the problem from a design standpoint, we must think of the character of the flower structure itself; that is, whether it is symmetrically petalled like the daisy, tubular like the morning glory, clustered like the larkspur, or completely odd as in the case of the jack-in-the-pulpit. We must think of its nature. Is it common or rare, dignified or slightly rowdy? Is it jolly, bright, dainty, shy, innocent, pert, or saucy? Tradition and taste have created so much symbolism in our use of flowers that to draw on that common acceptance of spirit will ensure sympathetic interpretation of flower character from an audience. Color, texture, and a suggestion of form which will be compatible with body structure are necessary considerations. It is helpful to think of the spirit of the flower as expressed in the dress and identifying forms used in hats or other accessories.

Very simple, sleeveless bodice dresses form a very good foundation for most flower costumes. Short tunics or little shirts and shorts of green material are also practical and delightful for the rollicking types. Over these foundations there may be added petals and leaves in the form of overskirt or collars. Sometimes a hat is enough to suggest a flower. Often a color scheme alone is sufficient, as, for instance, a group of full-skirted figures to suggest bluebells.

For the simple dresses, fine cotton or nylon net are desirable materials. For tunics, a muslin or similar fabric, easily dyed, is suggested. Sports shirts and shorts may be used for boyish costumes. For petals, hats, etc., crepe paper is excellent, although it is widely used for entire costumes. It is not a material recommended for dresses in this book because it is impractical for second use, and it is our proposition that most costumes should be made to serve several occasions.

DAISY

The daisy is typical of flowers petalled around a center. The short bodice dress is here used as foundation. The waist may be thought of as the flower center and treated in color accordingly. A yellow bodice with deeper yellow circles painted on it may be used for a white daisy, and a brown bodice with yellow rings, for a black-eyed Susan. The petals over the skirt can be cut of crepe paper or muslin. If crepe paper is used, cut it so the grain goes crosswise of the petal. A long flower wire should be sewn down the center of each petal so that it can be bent slightly. Stretch the tips of the petals a very little to straighten the paper. For a white daisy, a pale green or yellow skirt under the petals offers a subtle contrast to the white flower. For a black-eyed Susan with yellow petals, a white or pale green skirt is effective. A small cap (Juliet type) in brown or green is a delightful addition to the costume. Other flowers which may be developed on this plan are: tulip, bachelor button, carnation, marigold, rose, poppy, buttercup.

LILY

Since the lily is a flower of simple dignity and is tubular in form, a longer dress than the one for the daisy is desirable. The skirt may be gored in order to be slimmer around the waist and still have fullness at the bottom. The bodice should be tight-fitting and simple and should be green. Short petals of green (wired down the centers) may be sewn to the waistband, and curved over the hips to suggest a calyx. Other petals should be cut slightly longer than the skirt, and wired down the center so that they can be curved upward. A simple cap of green or yellow will repeat the color as an interesting added note. Other flowers interpreted in this way are: crocus, adder's-tongue, morning-glory, petunia, hollyhock.

FLOWER COSTUME

Here is a suggestion for a clustered flower solution. A simple bodice dress, with extremely full skirt made to stand out by hoops or crinoline underskirts, is used for this costume. This is attractive if made to suggest the Crinoline Period, with straight-cut bodice, shoulder straps, and ruffles at top of bodice and around the bottom of the skirt. Pantalettes will add to the period effect and quaintness. Ribbons carrying cut-paper clusters of the flower may be sewn to waistband or fastened to a ribbon belt. As an alternative, clusters of flowers may be painted or appliquéd on the skirt. A cluster of blossoms may be fastened in the hair.

Flowers which may be suggested in the general way are: larkspur, lily of the valley, forget-me-not, lilac.

CLOVER

This is one of the common, jolly types of blossom and can be appropriately suggested by means of a collar and cap. Using a simple green tunic or shirt with shorts, add a paper collar made of three clover petals sewn into the neck opening. A stocking cap forms a good base for the head covering. To this fasten loops of paper or folded cotton cloth about three quarters of an inch wide and four to five inches long. Loops should be sewn so as to completely cover the surface of the cap. They must have body enough to stand up; and if they are made of white material, color may be sprayed on them. Other flowers are suggested by the illustrations.

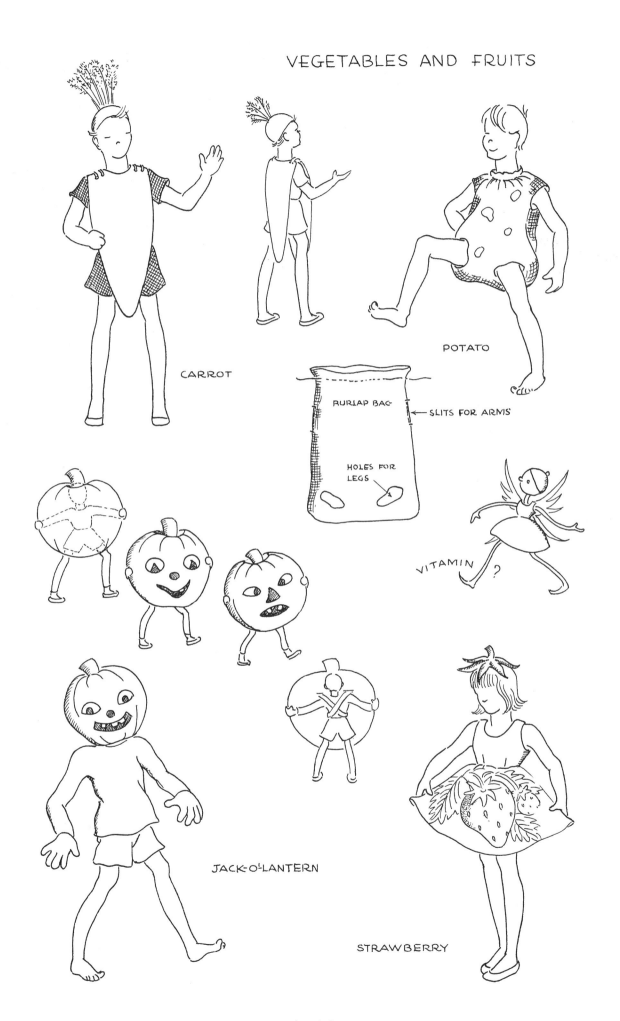

VEGETABLES AND FRUITS

CARROT

POTATO

BURLAP BAG ← SLITS FOR ARMS

HOLES FOR LEGS

VITAMIN ?

JACK-O'-LANTERN

STRAWBERRY

VEGETABLES AND FRUITS

HERE WE HAVE costume problems very similar to those posed by the flowers. To attempt realism in solution is to create almost total immobility, so once again we must think of emphasizing *character* and *color* rather than creating a reproduction of the vegetable or fruit.

Fruit and vegetable characters can be suggested without more than a passing reflection of the prototype. Color and action alone can be made to create an illusion. A group of children in bright orange tunics, with feathery green tops on little caps, can very well seem to be carrots, while green and white striped shirts, brown shorts, and small white caps may seem to say, "We are onions." Many, however, prefer a slightly more literal interpretation of character, and the following notes are offered to meet that preference. As in the case of flowers, the illustrations here included suggest types of costumes suitable for individual variation. The solution of the carrot, for instance, is applicable to fruits and other vegetables as well.

CARROT

The sandwich-board type of costume has many uses, but its ability to create a somewhat pictorial identification of character makes it desirable here. Beets, onions, apples, pears, and similar growing things of simple definite shape can be suggested by this method.

Cut two pieces of lightweight cardboard in the shape of the desired vegetable. Cut a hollow for the neckline, to allow the top of the cardboard to go well up over the shoulder. Fasten these pieces together by ropes or cloth straps. Be careful to have the cardboard shape not much wider than the child's shoulders and, if possible, above the knees in length; otherwise, freedom of arm and leg movements is very much hampered. The two pieces of cardboard may be loosely caught together just under the arm if very little movement is called for. This will help to round the figures a trifle. The shields may then be painted appropriately and a leaf or two of construction paper added where desired. In the case of the carrot, a cap made of an old stocking dyed green and topped with some feathery green spikes of cut paper will complete the suggestion. A foundation for this type of costume might be a green tunic, green shirt and shorts, or a simple green sleeveless dress.

POTATO

This very ordinary little fellow is often amusingly costumed by simply using a large burlap sack with slits in the sides for armholes, rough cuts made for the legs, and a drawstring a few inches from the top to pull it in around the neck. "Eyes" can be painted on. A note of caution: Wash the burlap bag first to rid it of some of its scratchy texture and its usual dust. Crumpled newspapers help to stuff it out.

Fit one bag as a trial, first, to discover exactly where to cut holes for legs in order to get the effect you want.

JACK-O'-LANTERN

Jack has become almost as traditional as Santa Claus, but his costume has not yet become as conventional or easy to procure. Until that happens he is variously represented as suits the fancy. He can be merely a simple little brown fellow carrying a pumpkin face on a stick. He may be pixielike, with pointed cap and a pumpkin sandwich board. He can be any quaint yellow-orange and brown thing. The illustration here is planned to show him with a paper pumpkin head made like a double mask. A long-sleeved brown jersey shirt and brown shorts would be a good body covering. For the pumpkin mask, cut two good-sized shapes from orange construction paper or other tough paper painted orange. These can be pasted or stapled together along the top half and pinned from the level of the ears to the shoulder, after slipping it over the head. Eyes, nose, and mouth should be carefully planned both for grotesque effect and for utility, since it will be necessary to have at least the inner corners of the eyes open where the child's eyes can use them. Likewise, the nose opening must accommodate itself to the actor's face. Strings inserted in the front of the face will tie around the child's head, making the mask secure. Some oversized orange gloves (work gloves dyed), firmly fastened to the wrists, will add to the grotesque appearance.

A parade of pumpkins, such as a chorus line might demand, could be amusing if large pumpkin shapes concealed all of the upper parts of the bodies. These can be made of large cardboard or beaverboard. There must be slits cut in the board at the height of the shoulders, and heavy tapes attached. These tapes cross the shoulders and fasten around the waist. This will help support the structure. The child must be able to hold the sides of the pumpkin with his hands. The straps should be loose enough to allow a slight turning of the body and head for locomotion. Since these figures are strictly two-dimensional, all movement would have to be lateral for a good effect.

STRAWBERRY

Similar to the costume for clustered flowers, this is one way of interpreting berries and small fruits. A simple dress with large, gaily-painted or appliquéd fruits is effective. The hat may suggest the stem or blossom of the fruit. Such a costume can carry leaves and beans or peas as well as berries. These may be of cut paper instead of being painted on. Overlapping layers of pale green crepe paper, curled back, may be used for cabbage. There are endless variations to this plan.

OTHER FANTASTIC CHARACTERS

WING

FAIRY

CLOWN

RUFF

JACK FROST

PAINT

OTHER FANTASTIC CHARACTERS

THERE are many odd characters called for in any listing of children's plays, which defy classification under the heading of Animals, Birds, Insects, and the like. While some of them were originally purely fantastic in conception and therefore costumed according to whims varying with locality and time, they have through years of traditional use become stereotyped in our thought. This stereotype has become so established that pattern companies are able to provide diagrams and directions for their construction. As cases in point, take Santa Claus, Pierrot and Pierette. Less rigidly conceived are such characters as clowns, witches, ghosts, and fairies. A third group of fantastic figures exists, allowing a fairly free play of our imagination. This group is composed of such indefinite characters as Jack Frost, Playing Cards, Fairy Tale characters, Cosmic Figures, and Vitamins.

SANTA, PIERROT AND PIERETTE

These old friends have become conventional. They are so familiar to us all in their usual representation that any great departure from tradition is unacceptable to the average audience. Several commercial patterns are available for these figures, and it is wise to use them and invent only in the matter of details. Let it be said that Santa belongs to the English-Speaking Union and that his counterparts in other cultures (St. Nicholas, Kriss Kringle) are delightfully varied.

FAIRIES

All that we demand of a fairy is femininity, daintiness, a pair of wings, and a sparkle. There are star fairies and moonbeams, frost sprites and spirits of gold and silver. There are wicked fairies and good fairies. But whether they be black or white, pink, yellow, or green depends entirely on the playwright's and costumer's imagination. Imagination demands access to light, delicate materials: gauze, cellophane, floating silks, and metallic sparkle. The illustration here presented is of the very simplest type and is designed around the bodice dress as a starting point. This should be made of nylon net or a similar fabric. The bodice should be lined in order to fit tightly. The skirt may be made of several layers of different colors. A good device for securing wings to the body is a strong but delicate-looking harness to be worn over the bodice. This consists of a waistband to which straps are attached. The straps are straight from waist to shoulder in the back, and cross over the chest. A light wire frame covered with thin plastic or other fairly transparent, delicate fabric should be sewn to a strip of material corresponding to the width of the straps. This can then be fastened to the harness over the backs of the shoulders. A delicate circlet or crown and a wand are traditional accessories. A star may be added

as ornament to the crossing of the straps in front. This star motif may be repeated as an all-over pattern on the skirt. The harness, circlet, and stars should be made of gold or silver cloth or painted with glue, and metallic sparkles sprinkled on while it is moist. Metallic sparkles a kind of ground glass, can be bought in paint stores.

CLOWNS

The traditional garment for the clown is a loose domino, and there are many standard patterns for it. It is fun, though, to experiment with all sorts of comic figures when clowns are called for. An exaggerated vest, built over an ordinary tightly-fitting one, creates an amusing deviation from the usual. Hobo clowns with too large pants and yards of suspenders are always humorous. A more European conception is based on loose, straight trousers cut as enlarged pajama pants, and a full hip-length smock top. This is decorated with large buttons or pompoms. A small, tight stocking cap with pompom covers the head. Distortion of form, exaggeration of make-up, and absurdity in material are keynotes to design for this figure.

JACK FROST

Jack was selected as an example of the wholly-imagined character. We think of him as sprightly, gay, and crisp. These are the qualities to get into his costume, however you do it. He could be any light, bright color, but one usually thinks of him as blue or grey or white. A simple hip-length tunic and shorts make a good foundation. If frosted with metallic sparkle, an elfin cap, round collar, and deep cuffs with points will prove a simple means to a lively appearance.

TOYS

To simulate these, actors are largely dependent upon action to create an illusion of the unreal; however, stiffness and distortion in costume will help. Toy soldiers must be very crisp in all costume details. Dolls should have unreal hair and strong make-up, with particular emphasis on eyes and cheeks to heighten the sense of unreality. Toy animals may be made of gingham, chintz, or some material other than the flannelette reserved for regular animal costumes. They should have exaggerated features.

PLAYING CARDS

Since a number of plays for children call for these characters, a word or two here may be of help. The solution may come in the ordinary use of the sandwich-board device, reproducing the cards desired; or one may dress the Kings, Queens, and Jacks in the spirit of the traditional card designs, which is definitely medieval, with angular emphasis upon all details.

DWARFS AND GIANTS

Disparity of size is here an important consideration. Everything possible in the way of making an unusually short tunic or skimpy trousers should be employed to *dwarf* a figure. Anything which can be worn to enlarge the appearance of the head, such as an oversized hood or cap, stuffed to increase its size, padded shoulders and long hair (to decrease the apparent length of the neck) will help to create the gnome or dwarf. For costume suggestion, see plate in section on Short Trousers, page 20.

Giants may use stilts if the action of the play permits. Under any circumstance all costumes should be planned to increase both apparent length and breadth of the figure. Padding, an enlarged false head, high-heeled shoes inside boots, a tall hat, and large gloves are all helps to this camouflage.

WITCHES AND GHOSTS

Witches' clothes fall into the group of costumes which has become more and more conventional. While a tight-fitting bodice dress, flowing circular cape, pointed hat, strings of hair, and vicious teeth mean *witch,* there is no reason why the witch must present a black silhouette. Red witches with yellow-green faces are startling; grey witches with green hair create a great surprise. A purple witch with auburn hair and strange symbols patterning the cloak can cause a gasp. We want to gasp at a witch, do we not?

Ghosts need not be sheet-draped figures, clumsy in movement. A slim white or light colored undergarment or tights may carry drapes of any semi-transparent material such as a marquisette or delicate plastic and will suggest the airiness we attribute to these other-world figures. This drapery may take the form of a large square, centered at the head and allowed to fall in long, free folds. It can be fastened to gloved fingers for security. The drapes need not be white. Try pale blues and greens as well as white. Luminous paint for accents will help to create a figure of fantasy.

STORYBOOK CHARACTERS

Alice in Wonderland, Robinson Crusoe, Snow White, and all the well-loved children and adults of the fairy tale and nursery rhyme are too well imagined by all of us to need much explanation or suggestion here. Children's storybooks themselves offer a wealth of illustrative material as source for costume inspiration. A word, however, must be said in warning. Be sure that your illustrations are consistent. Most artists conceive of fairy-tale characters as coming from the Medieval or Baroque periods. Don't mix them! A medieval prince and a Cinderella from the court of Louis XIV will never live happily ever after!

· Nursery rhymes are periodless and again, in costuming them, consistency is the only keynote. Any well illustrated *Mother Goose,* (many of them are in the spirit of today) may be a costume source. Story book illustration of an earlier time may have a distinctly early nineteenth century (Kate Greenaway) style. Don't mix the styles. Let Simple Simon and the Ten O'Clock Scholar be contemporaries.

PUNCH

PIERROT

PIERRETTE

HARLEQUIN

MASKS

A FUNNY FELLOW

3 DIMENSIONAL BEAR HEAD

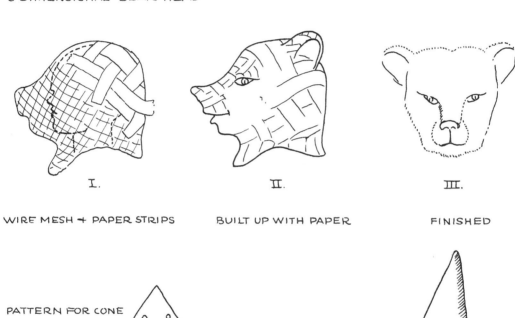

I.

II.

III.

WIRE MESH + PAPER STRIPS   BUILT UP WITH PAPER   FINISHED

PATTERN FOR CONE
USED FOR NOSE

PAPER BAG HEAD 1.

2a.

2b.

MASKS

THE USE OF masks in formal theatrical productions, especially amateur ones, is a highly debatable subject. There is no doubt as to the effectiveness of the well-made, well-fitting mask in heightening the grotesque, emotional, or humorous character of the professional play, in which it is usually employed with great restraint when used for an individual character. Mass effects such as those created by a dance group or chorus are often made more powerful if masks are used. For the nonprofessional play, and especially for a children's play, there are both advantages and disadvantages in using this device.

On the positive side of the comparison is the fact that many characters in plays for children are fanciful ones: animals, ogres, witches, and the like, whose representation is made easier if grotesque features are added. These features may be well accented if one has make-up and knows something of its application. Very often, however, this is not a possible indulgence, and the paper mask or half-mask comes to the rescue. A second advantage of the mask is that it has the psychological effect of destroying self-consciousness and thus becomes an aid to relaxation in the portrayal of a character utterly different from one's own. Negatively speaking, the mask, unless expertly fashioned (as it seldom is), can prove uncomfortably hot and a hindrance to movement, since it naturally keeps air away from the face and restricts a wide range of vision. These pros and cons must be balanced against the nature of the play and the kind of performance you are seeking.

Suggestions are here made for three kinds of face and head coverings which you may care to use. They are all fairly simple.

Other methods for constructing masks; other materials such as Celastic and cloth are presented and illustrated in the following books:

Alkema, Chester J. *Monster Masks*
Corey, Irene. *The Mask of Reality*
Cummings, Richard. *101 Masks*
Smith, C. Ray. *Book of Make-up, Masks and Wigs*

See: BIBLIOGRAPHY

A FUNNY FELLOW

Here is a variation on the paper mask as described in the section on Animals (page 67). The nose may be half of a hollow rubber ball, with pierced nostrils. This may be glued or taped on the mask. The hair is made of paper strips, curled by pulling them over the full edge of scissors.

HEAD FOR A BEAR

As an alternative to the flannelette hood for an animal costume, or as a way of making an unusually large head for a giant or other quaint character, the construction of a complete head covering is here offered. Some kind of wire cage must first be constructed, which will rest on the shoulders of the wearer. For this purpose, lightweight chicken wire (1″ mesh) is good. A piece 3½ to 4 feet square is approximately the right size. Bend it to fit around the back of the head first and down over the sides, curving with the shoulder. Shape the front to resemble roughly the general contour of the subject. Imagination must rule your construction. The wire can be pushed and wrinkled and snipped with tin shears. The broken ends must be worked in, as they might scratch the wearer. Roll under the outer edges.

The suggestion is often made that this framework be covered with cheesecloth as a second step. Others have found that strips of paper may be pasted directly over the wire by tucking the strip ends through the mesh. At any rate, cover the frame either eventually or at once with strips of newspapers (2″ by 3″ wide and about 12″ long) which have been thoroughly immersed in a creamlike solution of wheat paste (wallpaper paste). Apply the strips bandage-like on the diagonal wherever possible, overlapping them for secure binding. Tear the strips and use smaller pieces for detailed areas, such as around the nose and eye sockets. One layer may suffice for most parts of the head if you are careful. Build up the parts which require more modeling, such as cheeks, nose, lips, and forehead, by adding layers of bits of some paper pulp at those places. Be sure to secure these modeled areas to the foundation with surface strips. Ears may be modeled or made separately of paper (donkey's ears) and fastened on with paper strips. Allow the covered head to dry twenty-four to thirty-six hours, depending upon the thickness of the modeling. The paper will shrink and tighten during this process. When quite dry, the head can be painted with poster colors or scene paint. A coat of shellac will add to its durability. Features can be heightened by accented painting. Holes must be pierced for eyes and nose after the head is completely dry. Mouth openings will help to let in air which the actor needs desperately!

The wire head should be wrapped with cloth on its lower edge for the comfort of the wearer. It can be worn under the disguising garment if the neck allows for it. Or it can be put over the undergarment and a roll of cloth matching the foundation used to secure it to the base. Safety pins may be used, or a heavy thread (doubled) may catch the head to the undergarment. If possible, arrange the fastening so the head can be removed while the actor is off stage.

PAPER BAG MASK

These are fun for children to make and a practical solution to many grotesque demands. Use a fairly large brown paper bag and fit it down over the head of the actor, marking with chalk the correct position for eyes, nose, and mouth. Cut openings for these. Crumple the bag end in around the wearer's neck to mark the chin line. Remove the bag, and with paint or cut paper decorate the face as you wish. Long strips of paper or rug yarn make excellent hair. Curled paper can form good beards and mustaches. Flapping ears and strange noses are fun to experiment with. The nose may be a cone of paper with two holes in it, fastened on in the usual manner of slashing and bending back to fit a curve. Hats may be pinned or sewn on to these rude masks. Brown paper is pretty tough and will take a surprising amount of denting and wrinkling by way of shaping the face a little. The bag is simply tied around the neck with a string to hold it in place.

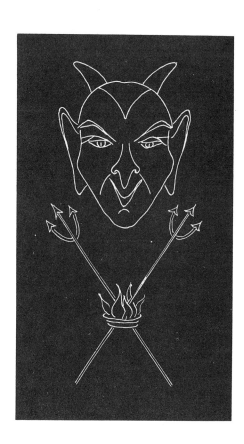

ORNAMENT AND ACCESSORIES

BECAUSE so often we may need a border design, a special reticule, or a particular style of apron rather than an entire costume to suggest period and place, the following pages have been included. Frequently we have on hand garments which adapt themselves easily to a number of periods, and the simple application of a peasant border, for instance, is all that is needed to imply a specific setting. Again, we may want to apply such a design to a tablecloth, curtain, or screen rather than to build a complete stage set. For classroom purposes and, indeed, often for public performance, this is sufficient to establish the scene of the play.

The following pages, therefore, include not only ornamental motifs from a number of periods and nations, but also a few of the typical utensils and accessories used as "props." The same bowl or bench can be used a dozen times over if given a fresh coat of paint and decorated in the style of the drama or story. While the following suggestions are by no means exhaustive, they are offered in the hope that they will provide that kind of detail which enhances an elaborate production or merely suggests a simple one.

GREEK ORNAMENT AND ACCESSORIES

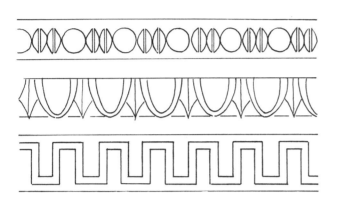

DECORATIVE BORDERS

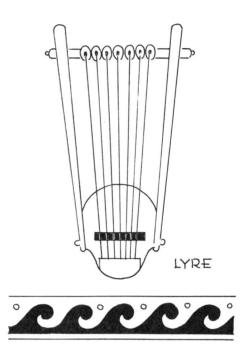

LYRE

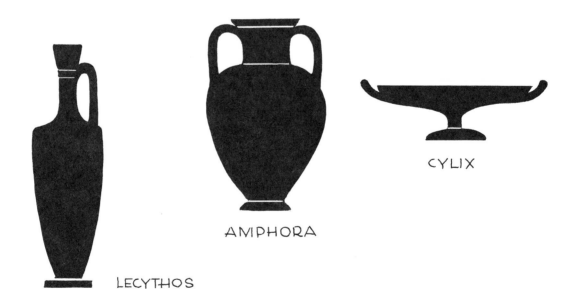

LECYTHOS

AMPHORA

CYLIX

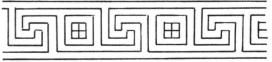

GREEK ACCESSORIES

HEADDRESSES

UMBRELLA

CRATER

FAN

BRACELET

FIBULA

FIBULA

ORNAMENT AND ACCESSORIES   500-1000 A.D.
ANGLO-SAXON, CELTIC, NORSE.

LANCE HEAD

SWORD

SCABBARD

SHIELD

KNIFE

AXE HEADS

MANTLE PINS

FIBULA

BROOCH

GIRDLE

HELMETS

LEATHER JERKIN
WITH METAL TRIM

CROSS

UTENSILS

CAULDRON

BRONZE
BOWL

BRONZE BUCKET

DRINKING HORN

MEDIEVAL ACCESSORIES

SHIELDS

POLE AXE

LANCE

CROZIER

BANNER

PENNON

CROWN

CHALICE

CROWN

MEDIEVAL ORNAMENT AND ACCESSORIES

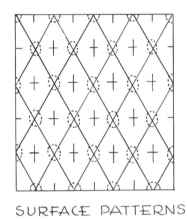

SURFACE PATTERNS

BORDERS

13 CENT.

14 CENT.

HEADDRESSES

GIRDLES

NORTH AMERICAN INDIAN MOTIFS

GOURD
RATTLES

BEADWORK AND WEAVING

BEADWORK

POTTERY

BASKETRY

WEAVING

LATIN-AMERICAN ORNAMENT

MEXICAN

MEXICAN TILES

PERUVIAN

GUATEMALAN

EUROPEAN PEASANT MOTIFS

NORWEGIAN

NORWEGIAN STAR

NORWEGIAN EMBROIDERY

SWISS PAINTED BORDER

GERMAN CANDLESTICK

CZECHOSLOVAKIAN EMBROIDERY

CZECHOSLOVAKIAN

EUROPEAN PEASANT MOTIFS

GERMAN

HUNGARIAN

FRENCH

HUNGARIAN

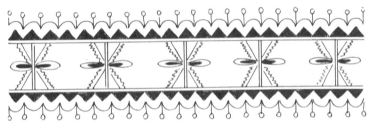

RUSSIAN

BIBLIOGRAPHY

Alkema, Chester J. *Monster Masks.* New York: Sterling Publishing Company, Inc., 1973

Barton, Lucy. *Costuming the Biblical Play.* Boston, Massachusetts: Walter Baker Company, 1937

Barton, Lucy. *Historic Costume for the Stage.* Boston, Massachusetts: Walter Baker Company, 1935

Bradshaw, Angela. *World Costumes.* New York: The Macmillan Company, 1952

Bucknell, Peter A. and Hill, Margot Hamilton. *The Evolution of Fashion.* New York: Van Nostrand Reinhold, 1973

Cordry, Donald and Dorothy. *Mexican and Indian Costumes.* Austin, Texas: University of Texas Press, 1968

Corey, Irene. *The Mask of Reality.* An Approach to Design for Theatre. Anchorage, Kentucky: Anchorage Press, 1968

Corson, Richard. *Fashions in Hair.* New York: Hastings House, Publishers Inc., 1965

Cummings, Richard. *101 Masks.* New York: David McKay Company, Inc., 1970

Davenport, Millia. *The Book of Costume.* New York: Crown Publishers, 1948

Ewing, Elizabeth. *History of 20th Century Fashions.* New York: Charles Scribner's Sons, 1974

Jackson, Sheila. *Simple Stage Costumes* and How to Make Them. New York: Watson-Guptill Publications, 1970

Johanson, R. Broby. *Body and Clothes.* New York: Reinhold Book Corporation, 1968

Laver, James (Ed.). *Costumes of the Western World.* New York: Harper and Brothers, 1951

Mann, Kathleen. *Peasant Costume in Europe.* New York: The Macmillan Company, 1935

Motley. *Designing and Making Stage Costumes.* New York: Watson-Guptill Publications, 1974

Purdy, Susan. *Costumes for You to Make.* Philadelphia: J. B. Lippincott Companuy, 1971

Smith, C. Ray (Ed.) *Book of Make-up, Masks and Wigs.* Emmaus, Pennsylvania, Rodale Press Inc., 1974

Snook, Barbara. *Costumes for Children.* Newton, Massachusetts: Charles T. Branford Company, 1970

Tilke, Max. *Costume Patterns and Designs.* New York: Hastings House, 1974

Walkup, Fairfax Proudfit. *Dressing the Part.* New York: F. S. Crofts, 1945

Wilcox, R. Turner. *Folk and Festival Costume of the World.* New York: Charles Scribner's Sons, 1965

Worrell, Estelle A. *Early American Costume.* Harrisburg, Pennsylvania: Stackpole Books, 1975

INDEX

Aba, 13
Accessories, 6, 7, 33, 87-93
Alpine peasant. *See* Bavarian; Swiss;
    Tyrolese
Amazon, tunic for, 9, 11
Angel, tunic for, 13
Animal
    basic garment, 65
    See also Bear Mask; Elephant; Frog;
      Lion
Antennae, 72, 73
Appliqué, 5
Apron, 6, 34, 36, 37, 41
Armor, 52, 53

Ballet dress, 36, 37
Bavarian, costume for, 20, 21
Bear mask, 82, 83
Belt, for stage use, 6
Birds, costumes for, 70, 71
Bishop, costume for, 50, 51
Bliaut, 8, 9, 13
Blouse and bodice, 40-43
Bodice, 38-43
    Breton, 38, 42, 43
    Italian, 38, 40, 41
    Mexican, 40, 41
    Polish, 38, 42, 43
    Swedish, 40, 41
    Tyrolean, 38, 40, 41
Bodice dress, 34-37
Bolero
    Czechoslovakian, 22, 26, 27
    gypsy, 22, 26, 27
    Hungarian, 27
    Mexican, 26, 27
    pirate, 22, 26, 27
Bonnet, 58-59, 60
Boots, 62, 63
Breeches, 16, 17, 20, 21
Breton
    bodice, 38, 42, 43
    child, 44
    smock, 42, 43
Butterfly, costume for, 72, 73

Cap
    French maid's, 54, 55
    mob, 54, 55
    nurse's, 54, 55
Cape, 48-51
    bishop's, 50, 51
    monk's, 50, 51
    Saxon and Norse, 48, 49
    seventeenth century, 50, 51
    sixteenth century, 50, 51
Carrot, costume for, 76, 77
Cat ear, construction of, 68, 69
Cat stair, construction of, 66, 67
Cavalier, boots for, 64
Celts
    costume for, 10, 11
    ornament and accessories, 88-89
Cheesecloth, uses for, 3, 13
Chinese, costume for, 14, 15, 18, 19

Fisher woman, 44, 45
Flower, costumes for, 74, 75
    See also Clover; Daisy; Lily; Nastur-
      tium; Sweet Pea; Violet
Footgear, 62-64
French fisherman. *See* Breton
French maid's cap, 54, 55
Frog, costume for, 66, 67
Frontiersman, costume for, 18, 19
Fruit, costumes for, 76, 77

Gaiter boot, 62, 64
Ghost, costume for, 80
Giant, costume for, 80
Godey's Ladies' Book, 37
Greave, construction of, 62, 63
Greek
    Chiton, 8, 9, 10, 11, 12, 13
    headdress, 13, 87
    ornaments and accessories, 86, 87
Gypsy, costume for, 26, 27

Halo, construction of, 54, 55
Hardware, as ornament, 6
Hat, 55
Headdress, 55-61, 87-91
Hebrew, costume for, 12, 13
Helmet
    insect helmet, 72, 73
    Norse and Saxon, 60, 61, 89
    Roman, 61
    warrior, 89
Hennin, 60, 61
Hoop skirt, 36, 37

Indian
    headdress, 56, 57
    motif, 19, 92
    trousers, 18, 19
    tunic, 13, 18
Insects, costumes for, 72, 73
Irish peasant, 44, 45
Italian bodice, 38, 40, 41

Jacket, 28-31
    boy of 1800, 30, 31
    Dutch, 28, 29, 30, 31
    Polish, 30, 31
    Tyrolean, 28, 29, 30, 31
    See also Bolero
Jack Frost, costume for, 79, 80
Jack-o'-lantern, 76, 78
Jack the Giant Killer, 13
Jerkin, 9, 11, 13, 91
Jester, costume for, 52, 53
Juggler of Notre Dame, The, 51

Kimono, Japanese, 13
Knight, costume for, 52, 53

Latin-American ornament, 93
Leggings, 63
Leg shields, 62, 63
Leotard, 11
Lily, costume for, 74, 75

Chiton, 8, 9, 10, 11, 12, 13
Choir boy, commercial pattern for, 2
Clergy, costume for, 50, 51, 64
Cloak, 47, 50, 51
Clover, costume for, 74, 75
Clown, costume for, 78, 79
Coat, 47
Colonial period
    boots, 64
    Puritan hat, 56, 57
    Puritan trousers, 20, 21
    vest, 22, 23, 24, 25
    woman's dress, 32, 33, 36, 37
Color
    changes through dyeing, 5
    Chinese, 15
    Dutch, 31
    Mexican, 45
    superimposed, 5
Coolie hat, 60, 61
Costumes
    permanent collection of, 1
    rental of, 47
Crayon, on fabric, 5
Cross-gartering, 11, 63
Crown, construction of, 56, 57, 90
Czechoslovakian, costume for, 22, 23,
    26, 27

Daisy, costume for, 74, 75
Danish peasant, 20, 21
Design, on fabric, 5
Dr. Denton garment, 65
Domino, 2, 17, 81
Doublet, 22, 23
Dress. *See* Colonial period; Medieval
    period; Nineteenth century;
    Romantic period
Dutch
    cap, 58, 59
    jacket, 28, 29, 30, 31
    trousers, 17, 21
    woman's dress, 34, 35
Dwarf, costume for, 20, 21, 80
Dyeing, 3, 4, 5
Dye powder, 5
Dye resistant, 5
Dyes, 4, 5

Ears, construction of, 68, 69
Elephant, costume for, 66, 67
Eton jacket, 31

Fabric
    design on, 5
    draped, 3
    dyeing of, 4, 5
    for general use, 3, 4
    simulated, 1, 2, 4, 5
    spraying of, 4, 5
Fairy, costume for, 78, 79
Fantastic characters, 64-81
Fez, 13
Fibula, 11, 88
Fichu, 32, 33, 36, 37

Lion, costume for, 66, 67

Madonna, costume for, 52, 53
Mantle, rectangular, 48, 49
Masks, 82-84
    construction of, 82-84
    use in theatre, 83
Material. See Fabric
Medieval period
    bliaut, 9
    cape, 50, 51
    headdress, 60, 61
    king, 12, 13
    ornament and accessories, 90-91
    page boy, 10, 11
    peasant, 13, 18, 19, 63
    queen, 12, 13
Mexican
    blouse, 40, 41
    bolero, 26, 27
    ornament, 93
    woman, 44, 45
Military uniform, 17
Mob cap, 54, 55
Moccasin, 11, 62, 63
Monk, costume for, 50, 51
Mother Goose, 37, 57
Motif, 5, 92, 94, 95
Musketeer, costume for, 50, 51
Muslin
    dyeing of, 4, 5, 75
    for angel costume, 13

Nasturtium, costume for, 74
Nineteenth century
    vest, 24, 25
    woman's dress, 36, 37
    See also Romantic period
Nomad, headcloth for, 13
Norse
    ornament and accessories, 88-89
    warrior, 60, 61, 63
Nun, tunic for, 51
Nursery rhyme costume, 80
Nurse's cap, 54, 55

Ornament and accessories, 85-95

Page, medieval, 10, 11
Paint
    crayon, 5
    poster, 5
    surfacing of fabric, 5
    textile, 5
Pannier, 32, 33, 36, 37
Paper-bag mask, 66, 67, 82, 83, 84
Paper cambric, 3
Pattern
    general suggestions, 2
    on fabric, 5
Peasant
    bonnet, 59
    French, 42, 43, 45
    jacket, 22, 23, 26, 27
    motif, 94-95
    Polish, 44, 45
    skirt, 45
    Swiss, 44, 45
    trousers, 17, 18, 19, 20

tunic, 11
    Tyrolean, 34, 35
Peter Piper, 13
Pierrot and Pierrette, 79, 81
Pioneer
    man's costume, 18, 19
    woman's costume, 34, 35
Piper's Son, jerkin for, 9
Pirate, costume for, 22, 23, 26, 27
Pixie, costume for, 20, 21
Plaid, creating effect of, 5
Playing card characters, 79, 80
Poke bonnet, 60, 61
Polish costume
    bodice, 38, 39, 42, 43
    bolero jacket, 22, 23
    jacket, 30, 31
    woman's, 44, 45
Poster paint, on fabric, 5
Potato, costume for, 76, 77
Prince, jerkin for, 9
Prince Albert, 24, 25
Properties, stage, 85-91
Punch, 80
Puritan
    coat, 47
    collar, 32, 33
    hat, 56, 57
    trousers, 16, 17, 20, 21
    woman, 36, 37
Puss in Boots, 64

Quaker
    bodice dress, 37
    trousers for, 21

Rabbit ear, construction of, 68, 69
Rebosa, 44, 45
Rental of costumes, 47
Roman helmet, 60, 61
Romantic period
    boy's jacket, 30, 31
    woman's dress, 34, 35
Rooster, costume for, 70, 71
Russian
    bodice, 39, 42, 43
    tunic blouse, 42

Sandal, 11, 62, 63
Saxon
    ornament and accessories, 88-89
    tunic, 8
    warrior, 10, 11
Scandinavian, costume for, 20, 21
Scapular, 51
Seventeenth century cape, 50, 51
Shawl, 6
Shepherd, costume for, 8, 9, 10, 11
Shield, 52, 88, 89
Shoes. See Footgear; Moccasin; Sandal
Simple Simon, 13
Sixteenth century
    cape, 50, 51
    jerkin, 9
    knight, 53
Skirt, 44-47
    Breton, 44
    Irish, 44, 45
    Mexican, 44, 45

Polish, 44, 45
    semicircular, 46, 47
    straight, 44, 45
    Swiss, 44, 45
    used as cape, 48, 49
Sleevelet, 12, 13, 36, 37
Slippers, 63
Smock, French fisherman's, 42, 43
Soldier, 17, 47
    See also Toy soldier
Spanish cape, 50, 51
Spanish dancer, 18, 19
Spraying
    of fabrics, 4, 5
    poster paint used in, 5
    stencils used in, 5
Stage properties, 85-91
Stencil, 5
Storybook characters, 80
Strawberry, costume for, 76, 77
Stripes, creating effect of, 5
Sunbonnet, 58, 59
Surcoat, 52, 53
Surface decoration, 5
Swedish bodice, 40, 41
Sweet pea, 74, 75
Swiss peasant, 44, 45

Textile designer, 5
Textile paint, 5
Theatre, 1, 3, 4
Toy, costumes for, 79
Toy soldier, 18, 19
Trousers
    Bavarian, 20, 21
    Chinese, 18, 19
    Dutch, 16, 17
    dwarf, 20, 21
    frontiersman, 18, 19
    Indian, 18, 19
    long, 18, 19
    peasant, 18, 19, 20, 21
    pixie, 20, 21
    Puritan, 16, 17, 20, 21
    Revolutionary period, 17
    short, 20, 21
    Spanish dancer, 18, 19
    toy soldier, 18, 19
    Turkish, 17
    See also Breeches
Tunic, 8-13
    fabrics for, 11
    long, 12, 13
    short, 8, 11
Turk, trousers for, 17
Tyrolese, 28, 29, 30, 31, 38, 40, 41

Uncle Sam, 2, 17

Vegetable, costumes for, 76-77
Vest, 22-25
Victorian dress, 36, 37
Violet, costume for, 74, 75

Waistcoat, 25
Wing, construction of, 70, 71
Witch, costume for, 37, 57, 80, 82

Zany, 53